Japan,
the United States
and a
Changing Southeast Asia

The Asia Society is a nonprofit, nonpolitical public education organization dedicated to increasing American understanding of Asia and its growing importance to the United States and to world relations. Founded in 1956, the Society covers all of Asia—22 countries from Japan to Iran and from Soviet Central Asia to the South Pacific islands. Through its programs in contemporary affairs, the fine and performing arts, and elementary and secondary education, the Society reaches audiences across the United States and works closely with colleagues in Asia.

The *Asian Agenda* program of The Asia Society seeks to . . .

- Alert Americans to the key Asian issues of the 1980s
- Illuminate the policy choices facing decision-makers in the public and private sectors
- Strengthen the dialogue between Americans and Asians on the issues and their policy implications.

The issues are identified in consultation with a group of advisors and are addressed through studies and publications, national and international conferences, public programs around the U.S., and media activities. The Asian Agenda program is currently supported by grants from the Rockefeller Foundation, the Ford Foundation, the Andrew W. Mellon Foundation, the Henry Luce Foundation, the Rockefeller Brothers Fund, and the United States-Japan Foundation.

Responsibility for the facts and opinions expressed in this publication rests exclusively with the author. His opinions and interpretations do not necessarily reflect the views of The Asia Society or its supporters.

Japan,
the United States
and a
Changing Southeast Asia

Charles E. Morrison

UNIVERSITY
PRESS OF
AMERICA

LANHAM • NEW YORK • LONDON

THE
ASIA
SOCIETY

All University Press of America books are produced on acid-free
paper which exceeds the minimum standards set by the National
Historical Publications and Records Commission.

FOREWORD

Japan and the United States have developed a unique partnership in the last generation. In spite of the differences of geography, history and culture, the partnership is widely regarded today as vital to the interests of both nations. Yet with the emergence of Japan as a global economic and political power, the partnership is being tested anew, sometimes severely. Americans now tend to focus on problems in the bilateral relationship, but in the years ahead both Japan and the United States will face challenges to their interests in regional contexts that will pose new demands on their partnership.

Asia is a prime theater for potential Japanese-American cooperation that could further strengthen their partnership. But it is also a region in which failure could have severe consequences for the security and prosperity of both countries -- and for their relationship with each other. Several changes in the region during the 1970s -- the shifting strategic environment, the opening of the People's Republic of China, the increasing significance of the Association of Southeast Asian Nations, and new threats to stability and security in Southwest Asia -- require adjustments in the perceptions and policies of both nations.

This report is part of a project on "Japan and the United States in a Changing Asia" organized by The Asia Society. The project, one of several under the Society's "Asian Agenda" program, is designed to foster increased American understanding and U.S.-Asian dialogue on the multilateral relations of Japan and the United States in Asia. The first phase of the project focused on the interactions of the United States and Japan with the nations of the Association of Southeast Asian Nations. The project's activities included a conference which brought together about 50 Southeast Asians, Japanese, and Americans from academia, government, business, and journalism in Hakone, Japan in July 1984. Co-sponsored by The Asia Society and the Japan Center for International Exchange (JCIE), Tokyo, in cooperation with the Institute for Southeast Asian Studies (ISEAS), Singapore, the conference helped provide a foundation for the analysis in this report. Another major component of the project, public programs in six U.S. cities in February 1985, allowed eight Japanese and

70973

Southeast Asian specialists to share their views of U.S.-Japan-Southeast Asia relations with diverse American audiences. Finally, the project attracted corporate attention to economic and business interactions through conferences on Japan's economic roles in Asia and the impact of Japanese financial liberalization on Southeast Asian markets. The second phase of the project on Japan and the U.S. in Asia, which has just begun, will explore their multilateral relations in Northeast Asia. A third phase, in 1986-87, will focus on South and Southwest Asia.

This report is also significant in that it is the first to emerge from The Asia Society's new national public education program on contemporary Asian affairs, "America's Asian Agenda." The Asian Agenda program seeks to alert Americans to critical issues in Asian affairs and in U.S.-Asian relations, to illuminate the choices which public and private policymakers face, and to strengthen trans-Pacific dialogue on the issues. Through studies, national and international conferences, regional public programs in the U.S., and corporate and media activities, the program involves American and Asian specialists and opinion leaders in a far-reaching educational process. Asian Agenda publications will emphasize short, timely reports aimed at a wide readership. Forthcoming Asian Agenda reports will treat topics such as Islam and Public Life in Asia, East Asia and the American Economy, and Christianity in Korea.

The Asia Society is indebted to many individuals and organizations for their contributions to the project on "Japan and the United States in Asia" and to the development of this publication. We are most grateful of course to the author, Charles E. Morrison of the East-West Center and JCIE, for committing himself so energetically and creatively to the task of reporting on a topic so broad and complex. We are greatly pleased by the result.

The Society's Asian collaborators and colleagues were indispensable to the project. We especially appreciate the extraordinary role played by the Japan Center for International Exchange under the leadership of Tadashi Yamamoto. JCIE generously allowed The Asia Society to draw upon its long-standing "Asian Dialogue" program in constructing the international conference and brilliantly organized that conference. As a cosponsor of the "Asian Dialogue," the Institute for Southeast Asian Studies, Singapore, directed by

vi

Kernial Sandhu, made possible the very stimulating Southeast Asian participation in the Hakone meeting.

In the United States several persons played key roles in the development of the project on Japan and the United States in a Changing Southeast Asia. Robert A. Scalapino of the University of California, Berkeley, and David D. Newsom of Georgetown University, co-chairmen of the Asian Agenda Advisory Group, guided our early thinking. Gerald Curtis of Columbia University provided valuable leadership as the chairman of the project's core group. Evelyn Colbert of the Johns Hopkins School of Advanced International Studies was a trusted adviser throughout.

The Asia Society is grateful to several foundations whose support made this project possible. The leading contribution was generously provided by the United States-Japan Foundation. We appreciate very much the interest taken in the project by the United States-Japan Foundation's President, Ambassador Richard Petree, and by its program director, Dr. Ronald Aqua. The Japan-United States Friendship Commission also took a special interest in this project. General program support from the Ford, Rockefeller and Luce foundations and the Rockefeller Brothers Fund was essential to the project on Japan and the United States in Asia as well as to the parent Asian Agenda program.

Finally, several members of The Asia Society's staff were instrumental in the development and execution of the project leading to this publication: John Bresnan, Ernest Notar, David Timberman, Susan Heinz, Sara Robertson, and Rose Wright.

Marshall M. Bouton
Director, Public Affairs
The Asia Society
11 January 1985

ACKNOWLEDGEMENTS

This monograph represents not original research but rather the integration and interpretation of information from numerous articles and conference papers that relate to one or another aspect of the relations among the United States, Japan and ASEAN. It is impossible to acknowledge by name the many Southeast Asians, Japanese and Americans whose original efforts were used. I do want to acknowledge, however, a special debt of gratitude to Dr. Evelyn Colbert and Professor Astri Suhrke who worked with me as a team on the task of integration. Their contributions so infused the final product that they should be considered as coauthors.

Dr. Colbert is former Deputy Assistant Secretary of State for Asia and the Pacific and is presently a professorial lecturer on Southeast Asian studies at the Johns Hopkins School of Advanced International Studies. She originally agreed to write a discussion paper for the Hakone conference mentioned in the foreword; it turned out to be so comprehensive that it provided much of the basis for this monograph. Her ideas and some of her language were incorporated here with little change.

Prof. Suhrke is an associate professor at the School of International Service at American University. Her original papers concerning ASEAN and the member nations of ASEAN provided the basis for several parts of the monograph, particularly in chapters II and IV. In addition, she shared with the author not an inconsiderable degree of mental agony over such questions as the structure of the manuscript, the topics and issues to be covered, and the degree of generalization, and her many constructively critical comments at all stages of the drafting process were invaluable.

Of those individuals who read and commented on the final draft, the many detailed suggestions of John Bresnan of The Asia Society and Columbia University were particularly helpful. Dr. Marshall Bouton, Dr. Ernie Notar, David Timberman and Sara Robertson of The Asia Society provided invaluable help from the planning to publication stage.

Finally, I gratefully acknowledge the support and encouragement of Tadashi Yamamoto, Founder and Director of the Japan Center for International Exchange; Robert Oxnam, President of The Asia Society; and from the East-West Center, Victor Li, President, Seiji Naya, Director of the Resource Systems Institute, and Douglas Murray, formerly Vice President and now Executive Director of the Trustees of the Lingnan University.

Charles E. Morrison
East-West Center
January 1985

TABLE OF CONTENTS

I. INTRODUCTION

This small book treats the relationships of the United States and Japan with the six rapidly growing countries in Southeast Asia -- Indonesia, Malaysia, the Philippines, Singapore, Thailand, and Brunei -- called the ASEAN countries because they are members of the seventeen-year-old Association of Southeast Asian Nations (ASEAN). Without doubt, the relationship between the United States and Japan, the two largest market economies in the world, is one with important global implications. No third countries are more affected by this relationship than the smaller East and Southeast Asian countries, including the ASEAN group.

If ASEAN, Japan, and the United States are pictured as three sides of a triangle, it must be remembered that there are vast disparities among these sides. ASEAN is the most populous, with 270 million people, compared with 225 million for the United States and 120 million for Japan, but it is by far the poorest. The gross national product (GNP) of the combined six ASEAN countries is about $200 billion, only a sixth of Japan's GNP and a fifteenth of the United States's $3,000 billion economy. For ASEAN, the United States and Japan are vitally important as suppliers and customers accounting for fully half ASEAN's trade, as providers of foreign capital, and as large powers whose policies and behavior have a dominant influence in shaping the international economic and political environment around ASEAN.

It is not surprising, therefore, that ASEAN policymakers pay a great deal of attention to economic and political developments in the United States and Japan. What will be the future growth rates in the two larger powers, which have a major influence on ASEAN export receipts? Will the United States and Japan maintain open markets, especially for the less sophisticated manufactured products that account for an increasingly larger share of ASEAN exports? Will the United States continue to have large budget deficits, keeping interest rates high and thus attracting capital that might otherwise go to ASEAN countries and increasing the costs of their borrowings? Is it possible, as some in ASEAN fear, that Japanese and American efforts to assist China will build too strong a China, which would be a

1

longer-term security problem for the ASEAN region and a vigorous economic competitor? Will Japan and the United States continue to give the ASEAN countries diplomatic support for their position on the Vietnamese occupation of Kampuchea? Will increased U.S.-Soviet tensions result in a larger military presence by both countries in Southeast Asia, and how would that affect the security of the region?

Given these kinds of concerns and their centrality to the ASEAN countries, their leaders are simultaneously seeking both to maximize their influence with Japan and the United States and to reduce their dependency on these powers. Regional cooperation through the ASEAN organization is designed to help achieve both these goals.

From the perspective of Japan and the United States, ASEAN is much less significant. In Japan's case, the ASEAN countries are Asia-Pacific neighbors and represent an area in which Japan has considerable influence, compared with much of the rest of the world. Some Japanese believe that there should be a special relationship between Japan and ASEAN. Nevertheless, it is the United States that is Japan's chief trading partner and foreign policy concern, and Japan probably has more concrete political and economic interests in Western Europe, China, and the Middle East than the ASEAN region. For the United States, ASEAN is more distant and ranks still lower among foreign policy and international economic priorities.

Still, ASEAN is of increasing significance to the United States and Japan for the following reasons:

- In economic terms, ASEAN is one of the fastest growing regions in the developing world. It is a potential showcase of successful economic development through market-oriented economic strategies that could be relevant for other developing countries.

- The ASEAN countries have increasingly become an important part of the international economy. Traditionally they have been suppliers of raw materials such as natural rubber, tin, copra, and petroleum, and they are now developing processing, manufacturing, and servicing

2

facilities. They host about $19 billion in U.S. and Japanese overseas investment and conduct more than $60 billion in trade with these two countries.

- The ASEAN countries sit astride vital sea-lanes, such as the straits of Malacca, Sunda, and Lombok, that connect the Indian and Pacific oceans. A huge volume of East Asia's seaborne trade travels these routes, including most of Japan's petroleum supplies.

- The governments of the ASEAN countries share with the U.S. and Japanese governments similar perspectives on many international political and economic issues, especially those of regional significance such as the struggle in Kampuchea. They are all anti-Communist in their domestic orientation, all have been friends, and two are U.S. allies. One of these, the Philippines, is the site of two major U.S. military bases regarded as crucial for the projection of U.S. power in the Pacific region and the Indian Ocean.

The United States and Japan, as global powers, have a continuing problem taking into proper account and appreciating the more regional perspectives of ASEAN. This raises challenging questions for U.S. and Japanese policymakers. What mechanisms are needed to assure that high-ranking U.S. and Japanese policy-makers are aware of the interests and sensitivities of the ASEAN countries and the impact of U.S. and Japanese policies on them? How can the U.S. and Japan reconcile requests from the ASEAN region for special trade treatment or a regional scheme to stabilize export earnings with their traditional position of treating all developing countries equally? To what extent should ASEAN preferences affect the U.S. and Japanese positions on a regional issue like Kampuchea or on a broader policy question, such as their relations with China and the Soviet Union? To what extent should the United States and Japan take into account particular human rights and social justice issues in their policies toward the ASEAN countries?

These are issues that have been dealt with by specialists in the U.S. Department of State, the

3

Japanese Foreign Ministry, and the trade and aid bureaucracies of the two countries. They have only rarely exercised the sustained attention of the secretary of state and the Japanese foreign minister, much less the president and the Japanese prime minister. With significant changes occurring within the ASEAN countries themselves and with the economic growth of the entire Pacific Basin and the corresponding tightening of economic ties among ASEAN, Japan and the United States, increased attention to the relationships within this triangle is needed both from the policy-making communities in Japan and the United States and from their publics.

The following chapter will describe changes in the ASEAN region. Next the interrelationships between ASEAN, the United States, and Japan will be examined. Finally, some current and emerging issues will be looked at in more detail. A word of caution is in order. The use of the terms "the ASEAN region" or "ASEAN" can give a misleading impression of a cohesive unit with unified interests and a central decision-making process. The reality, of course, is that there are six countries, within each of which there are many interpretations of national and regional interests. The ASEAN governments cooperate only in some limited areas; in many others they do not. For the sake of brief analysis, this complex reality must be simplified. Usually only dominant views associated with the governments are presented in detail. The reader, however, should be alert to the pluralistic nature of that region and societies being discussed here, a diversity that could be given fully adequate attention only in a much longer treatise.

4

II. THE ASEAN REGION: AN OVERVIEW

The economies and political institutions of the ASEAN countries have been strongly influenced by Western European and American influences dating from the colonial era. Prior to World War II, the modern sectors of the ASEAN economies produced primary products, minerals, and fuels primarily for export to the mother country and its trading partners, and the education of the indigenous elite was carried out in educational systems infused with European and American values. Even in Thailand, which had maintained its political independence, European cultural and economic ties were strong. In all other countries but Indonesia, sovereignty eventually was peacefully transferred to indigenous political and economic leaders who, although nationalists, had been nurtured on the values of the Western mother countries and saw it in their interests to maintain close and cooperative relations with the former colonial powers. No sharp discontinuity of basic institutions took place; the ASEAN countries remained integrated in the Western-dominated world economy, and their modern political and legal institutions were formally fashioned on Western models, though they gradually underwent transformation as events seemed to require. Only in Indonesia in the later years of Sukarno's rule was there a significant attempt to break with the West, and this effort came to a decisive end when the anti-Communist Suharto government was established in 1966.

Although change has occurred incrementally in the postwar years, cumulative change has been considerable. The ASEAN economies remain as integrated into the international economic system as before, but their main trade ties have shifted away from Europe, toward the United States and, most dramatically, toward Japan, which became the dominant external economic power in the region by the late 1960s. The composition of trade has also gradually been shifting away from primary products and toward more manufactured goods. The Western parliamentary and legal systems have been altered, generally to strengthen the powers of state and limit freedom of dissent, although not to the same extent as in many other developing countries. The sharp differences between the traditional elite, often educated abroad, and the rest of the population are gradually being

5

softened by the expansion of locally educated middle and professional classes and their movement into positions of some authority in government and the private sector. Diplomatic relations have also diversified away from the former mother countries and toward other Asian nations. The creation of the ASEAN organization is a manifestation of this. In sum, despite elements of continuity, the political institutions, the economies, the societies, and the international relationships of the ASEAN countries are undergoing fundamental change.

Political Stability

The ASEAN region has been characterized by a high degree of apparent political stability since the middle of the 1960s. This is reflected in the longevity of heads of government. Lee Kwan Yew has been the prime minister of Singapore since 1959, Ferdinand Marcos was elected president of the Philippines in 1965, and Suharto also became the effective head of state of Indonesia in 1966. In Malaysia there have been four prime ministers since independence in 1957, selected through elections and all from the same political institution, the United Malay National Organization. Only in Thailand during this period have there been frequent extra-constitutional changes in leadership, once in 1973 as the result of popular pressure, more frequently (as in 1976 and 1977) by coups. But there is also in Thailand an underlying continuity in the institutions of both the monarchy and the strong bureaucracy and in the enduring power-sharing arrangements between the military and civilians, although the terms are in constant dispute.

However, it is an open question whether the longevity of governments and leaders in the region should be regarded as a measure of stability or whether instead it reflects the absence of basic social consensuses that would permit more frequent alternations of power and signify longer-term stability. There continue to exist many of the basic sources of social and political tension that resulted, after the early period of independence, in the gradual abandonment of liberal democratic institutions modeled on European and American lines and the adoption of more authoritarian forms of control.

The central fault lines of conflict vary country

by country, but some generalizations can be made. One concerns the importance of ethnic politics in most of the ASEAN countries. Ethnic resentments are the principal source of social tensions in Malaysia, Singapore, and Indonesia, although in different ways in each of these countries, and there is little evidence that they are being significantly ameliorated. The potentially most explosive situation exists in Malaysia, where Malays account for approximately half the population, Chinese a third, and Indians most of the remainder. The only successful political parties have been ethnically based, with the ruling National Front (earlier called the Alliance) being a coalition of status quo oriented ethnic parties whose leaderships have struck a bargain with each other. This bargain essentially involves recognition by the Chinese party, the Malayan Chinese Association (MCA), and the Malayan Indian Congress of the primacy of Malay political leadership and of special rights and privileges for Malays in return for the protection of Chinese and Indian citizen rights, some cabinet positions, and a voice in government. This bargain is challenged by both Malays who would like an even more Malay or Islamic government and Chinese who believe the MCA has been too accommodative. The former, clustered in the Islamic Party (PAS), and the latter, based in the Democratic Action Party (DAP), have not been very successful in parliamentary elections, but the potency of underlying ethnic tensions, which they to some degree represent, led to the suspension of parliament in 1969-71 following severe communal riots, the adoption of constitutional amendments forbidding public discussion of ethnic issues, and the enactment of tough internal security laws. The New Economic Policy, designed to bring about economic equality among the races by 1991, is also a product of the 1969 riots. Some observers believe that, despite governmental stability, growing Islamic consciousness on the one hand and increasing Chinese dissatisfaction with what is seen as second-class citizenship on the other hand signify greater communal polarization below the surface of political life.

Malaysia's sensitive communal balance was the main reason for the separation of the largely Chinese city of Singapore from the Malaysian Federation in 1965. Singapore is run by the People's Action Party (PAP), whose leadership is provided largely by English-educated Chinese. The main political challenge has come from Chinese-educated Chinese, and

7

a major social fear is that, should communal violence
recur in Malaysia, it might quickly engulf Singapore,
where Chinese would be tempted to take revenge in a
city where they are the leading ethnic group. The
Singapore leadership maintains tight control over the
press and discourages open discussion of ethnic
questions regarded as potentially explosive. The
city-state's successful economic development and
social programs have helped consolidate PAP power; in
one twelve-year period (1968-80) the party swept four
general parliamentary elections before losing a single
seat to an opposition party in a by-election in 1981.

In Indonesia, there are some 300 ethnic groups.
The central ethnic division is between ethnic Javanese
who are religiously syncretic (abangan) and the
self-conscious Muslims (santri) of Java, Sumatra, and
other islands. Javanese have dominated the government
and the powerful military institutions. Indonesia has
had only two presidents, Sukarno and Suharto, in
almost forty years of independence, both Javanese from
the abangan cultural tradition. Sukarno abolished
Indonesia's largest Islamic party after some of its
leaders were involved in a rebellion in 1957, and
Suharto's government has forced the various Islamic
groups to merge into a single party that is watched
carefully by the government. The success of Iran's
Islamic Revolution has caused concern among the more
secular Indonesian leaders.

There are other expressions of ethnic tension in
Indonesia. The imposition of Javanese patterns of
administration in newer Indonesian possessions -- West
Irian, which became Indonesian in 1961, and East
Timor, which Indonesia acquired in 1976 -- has
aggravated separatist rebellions by the native
populations of those territories. There are also
occasional isolated instances of violence aimed at the
Chinese community, which is rich, small (2 percent of
the population), and relatively unprotected. The
willingness of some government opponents to criticize
the ties between government officials and some rich
Chinese businessmen and the sensitivity of the
government to such charges attest to the incendiary
quality of ethnic and economic resentment against the
Chinese. However, both the separatist rebellions and
the sporadic anti-Chinese violence are more a cause of
embarrassment than a present threat to Indonesia's New
Order government.

Separatist and autonomist sentiments also exist

8

among the Muslim minorities in the Philippines and
Thailand, both representing about 4 percent of their
countries' population and both concentrated in the
southern provinces of their respective countries, far
from the seats of political power. In the
Philippines, the rebellion led by the Moro National
Liberation Front with outside assistance from Libya
has persisted for more than a decade, at considerable
cost to the government, but neither it nor the less
serious Muslim unrest in Thailand threaten the
survival of the central government.

Aside from these historical ethnic tensions, new
sources of social and political instability arise from
the development process itself. This is not to imply
that without development the ASEAN countries would be
more stable, but it is clear that many changes
associated with rapid economic growth create new
political challenges, even as growth gives governments
greater capabilities. The ASEAN countries have had
small traditional ruling elites, in most cases the
landed aristocracy combined with newer elements who
rose in the colonial bureaucracies or, in Thailand's
case, in the military. Economic growth and the
broadening of educational opportunities have expanded
the middle and professional classes. In most of the
ASEAN countries, there has been an evolutionary
process of political adjustment involving the gradual
diffusion of political power, usually through the
representation of new groups in the legislative
institutions and their absorption into government
service and the military. In particular, the
professional "technocrats," whether coming from the
traditional elite families or the newer elites, have
been given prominent places in the ASEAN governments,
though their practical influence has varied, depending
on the willingness of political leaders to accept
technical advice. Singapore represents an extreme
case where a new elite group in the PAP and the
government has arisen principally on the basis of
educational and professional attainment rather than
traditional social status. In all the ASEAN countries,
however, the ability of the political systems to
provide some voice for newer social segments is a sign
of flexibility that should enhance stability. On the
other hand, there are still some groups not yet
incorporated into the political process. For example,
rapid social change and expanded education are
beginning to strengthen and make more articulate both
farmers and blue-collar workers, and it remains to be
seen how well the ASEAN political systems accommodate

9

these groups' future desires for increased political participation.

Violent challenges to the ASEAN governments from Communist insurgent groups have much diminished. Thirty years ago Communist parties or insurgencies were a serious challenge to most of the ASEAN governments. At present, however, all Communist parties are banned, and Communist insurgencies represent little threat, with the possible exception of the Philippines. In Indonesia the once very large Communist Party became moribund after the massive physical elimination of actual or suspected cadres in the wake of the 1965 coup attempt. The Malayan Communist Party was always disadvantaged by its predominately Chinese membership, and it has been driven into southern Thailand, where its remnants have broken into factions. In Thailand, conditions that would favor the growth of communism in the countryside, such as a landlord class, large numbers of landless peasants, and obvious rural poverty, are generally absent. Moreover, the Thai Communist Party has been weakened by bitter factionalism between the old Sino-Thai leaders, who stressed a rural-oriented, Maoist doctrine, and a new generation of cadres of laborers, students, and the intelligentsia who advocated a strategy keyed to indigenous conditions. Finally, the party has been a victim of the Sino-Vietnamese war. It was expelled by the Vietnamese from secure bases in Laos and Kampuchea because its leaders sympathized with China, but, because of the improvement in relations between the Chinese and Thai governments, much of Beijing's support also has been terminated.

Only in the Philippines has the Communist opposition grown in strength, reflecting the seriousness of current social, economic, and political problems in the Philippines as well as the ability of the Philippine Communist Party to fashion a strategy independently of external support or dogma. Estimates of the current strength of the party's military arm, the New People's Army (NPA), range from 6,810 (according to the Phillippine government) to 20,000 (according to the NPA). The NPA operates widely throughout the archipelago and constitutes a continuing drain on the government. Although not currently in a position to seriously challenge the government, the Philippine party does provide the one potential threat to an ASEAN government of a violent overthrow from an organization outside the existing political elite.

Political Institutions and Succession

The postindependence political institutions within ASEAN countries remain fragile and frequently controversial. Some of the longer-standing institutions in the region, such as the Philippine Congress, the two Philippine political parties before 1972, and civilian control of the military in the Philippines, have been swept away rather easily or seriously threatened. The political roles of such strong institutions as the Indonesian or Thai military are hardly universally accepted within these societies. Only Singapore and Malaysia have operated continuously on the basis of their original constitutions, although Malaysia's was temporarily suspended. Perhaps the most widely recognized and accepted institution in any country in the region is the Thai monarchy, which plays an important symbolic and ceremonial role in Thai society but does not govern. A central task of ASEAN governments is to develop and win legitimacy for modern political and economic institutions and to form a consensus on their societal roles.

The fragility of political institutions in Southeast Asia is particularly illustrated by the absence of effective or tested mechanisms for succession in several ASEAN countries. In Indonesia, the Philippines, and Singapore, the succession issue is an increasingly imminent one. In Singapore, the ruling PAP is consciously seeking to promote "second generation" leaders, but these are typically technocrats who have had little opportunity to learn political skills, given the absence of effective opposition. In Indonesia, the army provides a strong base for the rule of President Suharto, who was elected for a fourth term in 1983 at age 61. Unless Suharto himself arranges the succession, which he has shown no inclination to do so far, however, conflict within the army cannot be ruled out when he leaves the scene. The succession problem is most acute in the Philippines, where the legal and political institutions prior to martial law have been undermined or abolished. The army has not been an independent source of power, but an instrument of Marcos's rule. Morale is reputed to be low, and whether the senior officers beholden to Marcos for their advancement would be accepted in his absence remains to be seen.

11

The 1984 elections indicated that the democratic opposition has greater appeal and organizing capabilities than many had thought, but its relatively successful showing undoubtedly reflected more anti-Marcos feeling than pro-opposition support.

The ASEAN Economies

Governments in virtually all of the ASEAN countries have based their right to rule in large part on their ability to stimulate economic growth. Indonesia's New Order government of 1966 and President Marcos's New Society of 1972 both emphasized rapid economic growth. In Malaysia, the "New Economic Policy" has stressed the importance of growth increasing the incomes of Malays without reducing the incomes of Chinese.

The economic architects in ASEAN have been Western-trained economists or technocrats who have favored free enterprise, encouragement of foreign trade and investment, prudent monetary management and fiscal policies, increased domestic savings and investment, increased agricultural productivity, population control, and strong emphasis on the development of skilled human resources. Invariably the ability of the technocrats to put their programs in place has been limited by necessary political compromises, inadequate or corrupt administration, lack of resources, and external economic conditions. Nevertheless, compared to other developing countries, the ASEAN governments have generally pursued market-oriented development strategies effectively.

Levels of aggregate economic growth have indeed been impressive. Despite the oil shocks of the 1970s, growth rates in ASEAN have ranged from an average annual rate of 6.2 percent for the Philippines to 8.4 percent for Singapore, about twice the global average and more than a third higher than the average for non-OPEC developing countries. The global recession that began with the second oil shock in 1979 slowed ASEAN growth but did not reverse it. On the whole the ASEAN economies continue to expand more rapidly than those of most other developing areas and are growing at twice the rate of the industrialized countries. Only the Philippines has been an exception. If the future level of economic activity in the ASEAN region approximates that of the past decade, output will be tripled by the end of the century.

These growth rates have now pushed all the ASEAN
countries above the World Bank's low-income category.
At the top of the list is diminutive, but oil-rich,
Brunei, one of the richest countries in the world,
with a per capita income of approximately $20,000. In
1982, Singapore's GNP per capita stood at $5,900,
above that of such poorer industrialized countries as
Spain and Ireland. Malaysia's GNP per capita was
$1,840, more than South Korea's, whereas the
Philippines's and Thailand's stood at $820 and $800
respectively. Populous Indonesia has been the
laggard, having reached only the $580 mark in 1982.

The economic growth strategies of the ASEAN
countries have been strongly export oriented. Thus
dependency on foreign trade is very high compared with
that of the United States or Japan, ranging from 35
percent of GNP for the Philippines and 40 percent for
Indonesia to 100 percent for Malaysia and more than
200 percent for Singapore. The ASEAN group's trade
has been growing significantly faster than total world
trade, although it still accounts for only about 2.5
percent of world exports and 2.8 percent of world
imports.

Because of the importance of trade in the ASEAN
economies, they are highly vulnerable to changes in
the world market prices of their products and in
conditions of market access. Despite diversification
of exports, most of the ASEAN countries are still
mainly exporters of primary products and fuels.
Indonesia, for example, has suffered heavily from the
recent drop in the price of petroleum, by far its
largest export product. However, although primary
products will continue to be important, manufactures
are playing an increasingly important role in most of
the ASEAN economies. This mirrors the structural
change taking place in the ASEAN economies.

According to the World Bank's World Development
Report 1984, the proportion of national income
provided by agriculture in the four larger ASEAN
countries is in the 23 to 25 percent range. This is
down from 1960 levels of about 50 percent in
Indonesia, 40 percent in Thailand, 36 percent in
Malaysia, and 26 percent in the Philippines. The most
dramatic increases have been in the manufacturing
sector, which in 1981 provided 30 percent of national
income in Singapore, 25 percent in the Philippines, 20
percent in Thailand, 18 percent in Malaysia, and 12
percent in Indonesia. Manufactured products now

account for half of Singapore's exports (compared with 21 percent in 1960) and a third of the Philippines's exports (compared with 3 percent in 1960). However, in the case of Indonesia's exports, manufactured goods still account for only one percent. As the larger ASEAN countries move more into labor-intensive industries, where they have a comparative advantage, these will compete with some American and Japanese industries, and even more with the industries of such newly industrializing countries as Taiwan, South Korea, Hong Kong, and Singapore. Aware of this potential problem, Singapore is undertaking policies (restricting immigrant labor, increasing wages) designed to shift the economy away from labor-intensive manufacturing and toward more technology-intensive and capital-intensive sectors.

Socioeconomic Conditions in ASEAN

There has been considerable overall improvement in living standards in the ASEAN region, presumably resulting from development of the social and economic infrastructure including health care, education, sanitation, electrification, and expanded communications networks. In Indonesia, for example, data collected by the Asian Development Bank indicate that between 1970 and 1980 infant mortality dropped from 121 to 93 per 1,000 live births; persons per physician dropped from 26,510 to 11,530; the proportion of the urban population with access to safe water rose from 10 percent to 41 percent and the comparable proportion in rural areas, from 1 percent to 18 percent; daily calorie supplies increased from 1,970 to 2,450; literacy rose from 57 percent to 62 percent; and life expectancy at birth increased from 47 years to 53 years. As Table 1 indicates, the other ASEAN countries have shown comparable improvements in these measures of socioeconomic development, beginning from higher base levels.

The success of the ASEAN governments in promoting aggregate growth, however, has been much greater than progress toward a goal they all share in principle -- the achievement of much higher levels of social equity. Income inequalities remain large, except in Singapore. Estimates from the early and middle 1970s indicate that the richest fifth of the population received 49 percent of household income in Indonesia, 50 percent in Thailand, 54 percent in the Philippines, and 56 percent in Malaysia. The poorest fifth of the

14

TABLE 1: Selected Indicators of Economic and Social Development for ASEAN Countries*

	INDONESIA		MALAYSIA		PHILIPPINES		SINGAPORE		THAILAND	
POPULATION (MILLIONS, 1983)	158.06		14.74		51.96		2.50		49.51[a]	
TOTAL GNP (MILLION US$, 1982)	89,120		26,680		41,500		14,600		38,730	
PER CAPITA GNP (US$, 1982)	580		1,840		820		5,900		800	
REAL GNP GROWTH (1970–1980)	7.3[b]		7.4[c]		6.4		8.8		6.6	
	1970[d]	**1980[e]**	**1970[d]**	**1980[e]**	**1970[d]**	**1980[e]**	**1970[d]**	**1980[e]**	**1970[d]**	**1980[e]**
DAILY CALORIE INTAKE										
(CALORIES PER CAPITA)	1,970	2,340	2,530	2,660	1,960	2,320	2,800	3,120	2,260	2,310
DAILY NEWSPAPER CIRCULATION										
(COPIES PER 1000 PERSONS)	No Data	18	75[f]	174[f]	14	21	200	255	20	42
GROSS PRIMARY SCHOOL										
ENROLLMENT RATIO (PERCENT)	77	98	88[f]	95[f]	108	110	81	85	83	96
INFANT MORTALITY										
(PER 1000 LIVE BIRTHS)	121	93	41[f]	25[f]	60	55	20	12	75	55
LIFE EXPECTANCY AT BIRTH (YEARS)	47	53	64[f]	64[f]	58	62	68	72	58	63
LITERACY RATE (PERCENT)	57	62	58	60	83	75	72	84	83	96
PER CAPITA ENERGY CONSUMPTION										
(KG COAL EQUIVALENT)	116	220	582	838	263	328	1,261	4,219	183	371
PERSONS PER PHYSICIAN	26,510	11,530	3,700[f]	3,473[f]	1,157	1,136	1,522	1,222	8,450	6,839
POPULATION WITH ACCESS TO SAFE WATER										
URBAN (PERCENT)	10.0	41.0	100.0	93.0	67.0	66.0	96.0	100.0	60.0	49.0
RURAL (PERCENT)	1.0	18.0	1.0	4.9	20.0	33.0	N.A.	100.0	10.0	12.0
URBAN POPULATION (PERCENT)	17.1	20.0	27.0	29.0	32.9	36.0	100.0	100.0	13.2	14.0

Key: *Except Brunei.—[a]Preliminary.—[b]1971–1980.—[c]1973–1980.—[d]Data for 1970 refer to any year between 1968 and 1973.—[e]Data for 1980 refer to any year between 1976 and 1981.—[f]Peninsular Malaysia only.
Source: Asian Development Bank, Key Indicators of Developing Member Countries of ADB, Volume XV, April 1984, Tables 1, 2, 3, 4, and country tables.

population had only 7 percent of household income in Indonesia, 6 percent in Thailand, 5 percent in the Philippines, and 4 percent in Malaysia. These income inequities are not as marked as in Latin America, but are more so than in South Korea and Taiwan.

Despite the rapid growth rates, ASEAN is still a region of lesser developed countries with considerable, although often not very visible, poverty. The World Bank has estimated that in 1981, 41 percent of the Philippines's rural population and 32 percent of the urban population were below the poverty line. The corresponding figures for Indonesia were 51 percent and 28 percent respectively, and for Thailand 34 percent and 15 percent. The Malaysian government has estimated that 38 percent of its rural population and 13 percent of its urban population are below the poverty line. Overall, there seems to have been some decline in the percentage of population living below the poverty line (although, because of population increases, the absolute number of poor is probably increasing).

Expansion of the modern sector of the economy has accelerated urbanization in the ASEAN region. Excluding completely urbanized Singapore, the level of urbanization in the ASEAN region is still relatively low compared with other developing countries at comparable income levels. In 1981, the proportion of urban population ranged from 15 percent in Thailand to 37 percent in the Philippines, only about half the urban proportion for such countries as Peru, Colombia, Mexico, and Brazil. However, this should not be a source of complacency. Jakarta, Bangkok, and Greater Manila are already huge urban agglomerations of more than 5 million people, with serious problems of pollution, sanitation, slums, overcrowding, traffic jams, crime, and lack of adequate institutions to assist the destitute. These cities will have populations upward of 15 million by the end of the century, and providing employment, basic city services, and a minimally attractive urban environment will be a major challenge for the ASEAN countries. In contrast, Singapore, with its efficient government, high per capita income, small 2.5 million population, and ability to control inward migration, has provided the majority of its population with modern housing facilities and strictly controls traffic and maintains an effective campaign to keep Singapore green. Whether or not Singapore's urban environment, with its orderly rows of high-rise apartment buildings, is an

16

attractive urban environment, however, is also a matter of controversy.

Most of the ASEAN countries have succeeded in reducing birth rates. Success in introducing family planning is illustrated by the growth in the percentage of women using contraceptives, for example, from 8 percent in 1970 to 59 percent in 1981 in Thailand and from 2 percent to 48 percent for the same years in the Philippines, the two countries with the highest fertility rates. Although women are bearing fewer children, the high proportion of women of childbearing age assures that the ASEAN countries, already containing some of the most densely populated areas in the world, will continue to see their populations increase well into the twenty-first century. This means there is a continuing challenge to provide education, employment, and housing for expanding populations while seeking to make qualitative improvements in these areas.

Increased population pressure combined with higher standards of living places further demands on the physical environment of the ASEAN countries. For example, much of the increased food production has come from an expansion of agricultural land. In the process, cultivation has been pushed onto steeper slopes and into once-forested areas. Much new land is only marginally productive and, unlike the rich, arable land in Thailand's central region or the flood plains of Java, cannot sustain continuous cultivation for many years. Loss of forest cover increases the rate of erosion and adds to silt in the rivers. This clogs irrigation canals on which food production depends.

The search for firewood in populated areas and logging operations in more remote areas have aggravated the destruction of tropical forests in Southeast Asia. American and Japanese companies hold timber concessions in the Philippines, Malaysia, and Indonesia, but an even greater proportion of logging is done by smaller and medium-sized companies based in Korea, Taiwan, Hong Kong, and the ASEAN countries themselves. The ASEAN countries have regulations to protect their forests and safeguard other delicate environments, such as their marine resources, but these are often not effectively enforced. The main impact of the destruction of the natural environment will fall upon the people of ASEAN countries, but there are also global consequences such as atmospheric

17

and climatic changes associated with the diminution of tropical forests.

Some critics within the ASEAN region argue that such negative factors as income inequities, limits on right of dissent, and the destruction of the physical environment are systemic consequences of current development strategies. They believe that, rather than remedying these problems, further integration with the international economy dominated by Japan and the United States will merely aggravate them. The deep and visible foreign economic presence in the ASEAN region appears to these critics to support and reinforce existing social structures, with their economic and political inequalities. This is an issue around which nationalist and, increasingly, religious sentiment may be more effectively mobilized in the future.

External Security Concerns

During the past two decades, the security environment of the ASEAN countries has changed considerably. The Commonwealth military presence in Singapore and Malaysia came to almost a complete end in the early 1970s, and the United States withdrew militarily to its Philippine bases following the collapse in South Vietnam. The formation of a united Socialist Republic of Vietnam and the establishment of Vietnamese hegemony in Indochina have created a considerable security concern among the ASEAN governments, although there has been little concrete evidence of a threat so far. The Soviet Union, through its alliance with Vietnam and its use of naval facilities in Cam Ranh Bay, has established a new military presence in Southeast Asia, although it has little political influence in the region outside of Indochina. In contrast, China has succeeded in increasing its diplomatic presence in the region and is virtually allied with Thailand. Nevertheless, the ASEAN governments regard China, by virtue of its size, proximity, and presumed ties with local Chinese communities, as their most serious longer-term threat.

Security experts in the ASEAN region tend to define external threats in rather amorphous terms and differ about how seriously these threats should be evaluated. Clearly there is little perception that the ASEAN countries are about to be attacked or invaded by a country from outside the region. Rather, the most likely "outside threat" is externally assisted subversion or uncontrolled escalation of border skirmishes. There is also fear that conflict among larger powers outside the region might affect security within the region.

Vietnam and Kampuchea. The ASEAN governments probably were more anxious about external security threats in the period immediately following the collapse of the anti-Communist governments in South Vietnam and Cambodia in April-May 1975, than at any time in recent years. To adjust to the new external security environment, they sought to improve their relations with Vietnam and, in some cases, also with China as insurance (both the Philippines and Thailand normalized relations with China within three months of the fall of Saigon). In some ASEAN capitals it was felt that relations with Vietnam should be established for other reasons as well. Normalization of relations would symbolize and strengthen cooperation in Southeast Asia across ideological boundaries and help contain tensions that at least in part were seen as a result of competitive large-power intrusion in the region. This view was especially expressed in Jakarta, which had maintained a cautiously nonaligned position toward the war in Vietnam. The ASEAN governments also reinforced their own solidarity by planning the first ASEAN summit meeting, ultimately held in Febuary 1976.

The anxiety in most ASEAN states subsided, however, as Vietnam showed little interest in fomenting insurgency elsewhere in Southeast Asia. Moreover, as the dispute between Vietnam and Kampuchea began to develop more openly, ASEAN initially benefited as both Vietnam and China, the latter backing Kampuchea, sought support within the region. When Vietnam invaded Kampuchea and sent the Khmer Rouge regime into exile in December 1978, and was subsequently attacked in turn by China in February 1979, it seemed that a balance of power was operating among the Communist countries. The predominant assessment in ASEAN governing circles was a welcoming of the Chinese check on Vietnam, although China's invasion of a smaller neighboring country also was seen as an uncomfortable precedent.

Led by the Thais, the ASEAN governments condemned the Vietnamese invasion, arguing that the violation of Kampuchea's sovereignty was contrary to the principles of international law and a threat to regional peace.

19

ASEAN successfully supported the Khmer Rouge regime's retention of Kampuchea's seat in the United Nations by overwhelming margins in annual votes on the issue. The Khmer Rouge's reputation for having committed genocide against its own people made it a questionable ally for ASEAN to support, however. The ASEAN foreign ministries made a concerted and ultimately successful effort to compel the Khmer Rouge to merge, at least on paper, into a coalition government with non-Communist Khmer factions under Sonn San and Prince Sihanouk in 1982.

Most critical of Vietnamese actions, of course, was Thailand, which had regarded Kampuchea and Laos as buffers between itself and Vietnam, or even as areas that potentially could be drawn into a Thai sphere of influence, as had been the case in earlier historical periods. Refugee camps were established along the Thai-Kampuchean border and came to serve as bases for Khmer guerrillas. Chinese arms flows to the guerrillas were channeled in part through Thailand, with the obvious acquiescence and presumed assistance of the Thai military. Occasionally, Vietnamese actions against the border camps have spilled into Thai territory, causing loud protests from Thailand and its ASEAN friends. Although there has been some debate within the Thai government and in the Bangkok press about the possibilities of reaching some compromise with Vietnam, the official policy continues to demand a complete Vietnamese troop withdrawal from Kampuchea and self-determination for the Khmer people through elections. This position is supported by ASEAN as a whole, most staunchly and vocally by Singapore. On the other hand, the governments of Malaysia and Indonesia are less inclined to view Vietnam as a threat; groups within Indonesia in particular see Vietnam chiefly as a potentially strong barrier to Chinese expansion. High-ranking Malaysian and Indonesian officials, including the Indonesian defense minister, General Benny Moerdani, have visited Hanoi seeking some kind of compromise, so far without success. Hanoi's position is that it cannot withdraw completely until "the Chinese threat" is removed from Kampuchea, which refers to Chinese pressures on both Kampuchea and Vietnam itself.

The Indochina situation has affected the security of ASEAN in quite another way -- through the massive outflow of refugees, especially in 1978-79. The Indochinese have left their countries by land from Laos and Kampuchea into Thailand and from Vietnam into

20

China, and by boats to Malaysia, Indonesia, the Philippines, and Hong Kong. About 1.4 million have come to the ASEAN countries since 1975, representing a large majority of the total outflow. This influx has caused local and even national tension in the recipient countries, partly because many refugees have been Chinese. Some ASEAN officials have accused Vietnam of deliberately touching off the refugee flows in order to destabilize its neighbors. The "boat people" are disturbing for another reason -- they remind Malaysians and Indonesians of their countries' proximity to Vietnam by sea and point up their inability to patrol their own coastal areas. ASEAN led a strong international condemnation of Vietnam in 1979, and Vietnam subsequently complied with requests that it reduce the outflow of people. The threats of some ASEAN leaders to repatriate refugees or refuse them entry evoked a massive international campaign to bring the refugees to "countries of ultimate asylum," assuring the ASEAN countries that they would be accepted in the United States, Australia, Europe, and elsewhere and would not be a burden on the ASEAN group. Today, outflow to the ASEAN region has been sharply reduced.

The Soviet Union. Americans and Japanese tend to regard the Soviet Union as the most likely source of external threat to their countries. For Southeast Asians, however, the Soviet Union has traditionally been a relatively distant power. Moscow's 1978 alliance with Hanoi and subsequent use of the Cam Ranh base facilities brought the Soviet Union closer to ASEAN. However, the Soviet Union does not maintain a high military visibility in the ASEAN region (e.g., by naval movements), and ASEAN governments cite the limited Soviet ability in the past to project its power into Southeast Asia beyond Indochina as evidence of Soviet weaknesses in the region. In particular, it is noted that the Soviets have failed to develop close relations with any insurgent groups within the ASEAN countries.

Not being seen as a direct and immediate threat does not, of course, mean that the Soviet Union is viewed with sympathy. On the contrary, ASEAN government officials express deep distrust toward the Soviet Union, and there is little goodwill outside official circles either. The Soviet Union has figured prominently in espionage cases in Southeast Asia, and Soviet embassy and commercial personnel are watched carefully by ASEAN government intelligence organizations.

China. Traditionally China has been viewed as an actual or a potential adversary of the non-Communist governments of Southeast Asia because of its support for local insurgencies and the association of China with overseas Chinese, regarded as a potential "fifth column" in much of Southeast Asia. These two elements tend to reinforce each other because, as already noted, the Communist insurgencies in Thailand and Malaysia are dominated by overseas Chinese cadres. Links between China and the local Communist parties have varied, ranging from moral support to the provision of training, radio stations, and matériel. The precise nature of these ties is uncertain, and conflicting assessments have been made, particularly in the context of partisan political debates.

Two ASEAN governments, Indonesia and Singapore, still do not have normal diplomatic relations with the People's Republic of China. Indonesia severed its relations in 1967, two years after China's alleged support for the 1965 coup attempt, and the Indonesian military continues to harbor bitter resentments against China. The Singapore government, wanting to demonstrate beyond doubt to its larger Malaysian and Indonesian neighbors that the island is not a "third China" despite its predominantly Chinese population, has stated that it will not normalize relations until Indonesia does, although it maintains economic and de facto political relations with China. Malaysia established diplomatic ties with China in 1974 amid great fanfare, but since then the relationship has not been a smooth one. The China relationship is controversial in Malaysian domestic politics because of that country's delicate ethnic balance. Moreover, China has not renounced party-to-party (as distinct from state-to-state) relations with the Malayan Communist Party, whereas Malaysia wants China to terminate any form of recognition.

In contrast, Chinese-Thai relations have become quite close and are even described by some observers as a "quasi-alliance" -- formed by their common opposition to Vietnam. The Thai government regards China as an important balance to Vietnam and a power which, unlike the United States in recent years, is willing to act militarily against Vietnam should the latter upset the military balance. The Chinese government appreciates Thailand's cooperation in maintaining the Khmer guerrillas on the Thai-

22

Kampuchean border, and, more generally, Thailand's diplomatic firmness in upholding ASEAN's refusal to compromise with Vietnamese ambitions in Kampuchea. In return, Beijing has terminated virtually all its support for the Communist Party of Thailand. Viewed in the longer run, however, Chinese motives are suspect even in Bangkok.

Southeast Asia as a Zone of Peace, Freedom, and Neutrality. Much of the ASEAN thinking about external threats from great powers is focused on spillover effects from large-power competition. For example, the Soviet Union is not seen as having intrinsic interests in Indochina but as having become involved because of its competition with China and, to a lesser extent in this instance, with the United States. Similarly, U.S. bases in the Philippines are there because they are part of a global U.S. strategy of "containment" of the Soviet Union. Southeast Asian strategic thinkers consequently see a threat to the ASEAN region in the escalation of U.S.-Soviet tensions. In the words of one Indonesian, increasing tensions and arms competition between the U.S. and the Soviet Union are seen "as a destabilizing factor, because they could increase the likelihood of conflicts in the Third World, including Southeast Asia." He also notes that the endorsement of the ZOPFAN (Zone of Peace, Freedom and Neutrality) concept by the ASEAN countries "is a manifestation of their desire to make the Southeast Asian region free from the conflict between the U.S. and the U.S.S.R., or between any other great powers."

ZOPFAN first appeared in a declaration of the foreign ministers of the then five ASEAN countries following a meeting in Kuala Lumpur in November 1971. The individual governments disagreed on the tactics, timing, and preconditions for achieving such a zone, as well as on the appropriate role for great powers in the region once the zone had been created; but they did agree in principle that ZOPFAN was a desirable objective. The concept expressed in part a nationalistic chafing over having to be dependent on large-power policies beyond their control, even though some of these policies were generally supportive of the ASEAN governments, for example, those of the U.S. and Japan. The endorsement of ZOPFAN at the time was also intended to provide needed political support for the new Malaysian prime minister, Tun Abdul Razak, who had proposed the idea. In the mid-1970s, the ASEAN countries tried to interest Vietnam in the concept,

but no agreement was reached. Although the
realization of ZOPFAN remains a long-term objective,
it is not now being actively pursued by the ASEAN
nations.

In the interim, all the ASEAN governments
maintain close and beneficial links with the Western
powers, Australia, and Japan. Four of them have
military ties with external powers: the Philippines
and Thailand are allied with the United States,
whereas Malaysia and Singapore are linked to Britain,
Australia, and New Zealand under the consultative Five
Power Defense Arrangements. Also, given the dominant
role of the United States and Japan in the ASEAN
economies, it is questionable if these countries could
become truly neutral. The nature of triangular
security relationships among ASEAN, the United States,
and Japan will be examined in the following chapter.

Defense Expenditure in the ASEAN Region. All the
ASEAN governments agree that "national and regional
resilience" should be the ultimate basis for their
security. This term, introduced by Indonesians with
reference to their own nonaligned policy, emphasizes
that if the ASEAN countries are able to deal with
internal sources of tension on a national basis and
through regional cooperation, they are in a much
stronger position to counter external threats.

Although national resilience is seen to lie
principally in economic and social development,
greater attention has been given to military strength
since the fall of Saigon. Although manpower has
expanded only modestly (Indonesia's armed forces are
the largest, at about 280,000), the growth in military
expenditures has been more rapid. In the Philippines,
average annual real military expenditures from 1975 to
1980 were about double the average annual expenditures
from 1970 to 1974. The increase has been justified
with reference to the growing activities of Communist
and Muslim insurgents. For the same periods, average
annual Indonesian and Malaysian military expenditures
increased by slightly over half, Thailand's by better
than 40 percent, and Singapore's by about one-third.
Much of the recent increase in Thailand has been
related to the tense situation in Kampuchea since the
Vietnamese invasion. The Malaysian government, which
likewise responded to the Kampuchean crisis by
announcing increased military preparedness (including
a major airbase to be built on the northeast coast),
has since scaled down the plans to conform with the

general austerity policies occasioned by the 1982 recession. It should also be noted that because GNP rose rapidly in the 1970s, ASEAN military expenditures have not increased as a percentage of GNP, remaining in 1982 at roughly 4 percent, the same as in 1975. Proportionately, Singapore spends the most on defense (almost 6 percent of GNP) and the Philippines the least (about 2 percent of GNP), suggesting that the relationship among defense expenditures, GNP, and security problems is not very straightforward.

There has also been a modest expansion of military cooperation among the ASEAN countries, including border cooperation, intelligence and information exchanges, some joint exercises by two or more countries, training exchanges, and the beginnings of some standardization of military equipment. These activities take place outside the formal ASEAN framework, and there is no desire among the members to transform ASEAN into a military alliance. It is recognized that to do so would not significantly enhance the countries' military capabilities and would be regarded as provocative by Vietnam.

The ASEAN Organization

The progress of regional cooperation among the ASEAN countries has been another important development in the region. Created in August 1967 by the original five member countries (Brunei joined only in January 1984), ASEAN's primary stated purposes were to enhance development through regional economic, social, and cultural cooperation. ASEAN was never meant to achieve regional economic integration, unlike the European Common Market, which has definite integrationist goals. Many of the economic projects associated with the ASEAN organization -- such as the trade preference scheme, large-scale industrial projects, and ASEAN joint ventures -- have been slow to get off the ground. The achievement of ASEAN, therefore, has been less in the economic field and more in the political and is one of developing a sense of solidarity among countries that previously were distant from one another or on occasion were in conflict. In this way ASEAN gave psychological reassurance to and symbolic support for the member governments, not as a traditional security alliance but as an association of friendly governments.

This was most clearly demonstrated by the

25

expansion of ASEAN activities in 1976. For the previous eight years, ASEAN had existed as an organization of foreign ministers; although many meetings were held and the groundwork was laid to build habits of cooperation among the five countries, there was a sense that little concrete was being achieved. To demonstrate their solidarity in the wake of the Vietnamese victories in Indochina, the ASEAN governments felt it was important to materially strengthen the ASEAN organization. The heads of governments were brought into the organization at the highest decision-making level, and their first summit meeting was held in February, 1976. Below them, the economics ministers were included formally on the same second-tier level as the foreign ministers and took over the management of economic cooperation. Agreement was reached to establish a permanent secretariat in Jakarta; before that ASEAN operated through national secretariat offices in each country. A Declaration of ASEAN Concord established a more specific program of cooperation, and a Treaty of Amity and Cooperation in Southeast Asia set out general principles for the settlement of disputes. Soon after, the economics ministers reinvigorated ASEAN's functional committees, established a program for reducing tariff and trade barriers among the countries, and agreed on a scheme to establish large-scale industrial projects.

In the later 1970s and early 1980s, much of the early momentum of economic cooperation was lost, because many practical difficulties were encountered when the governments tried to further elaborate and implement their plans. However, following the Vietnamese invasion of Kampuchea, there was a new demonstration of utility of ASEAN, this time on the diplomatic and political level. The ASEAN governments' ability to fashion a common agenda and their repeated successes in U.N. votes on Kampuchea and in marshaling U.S. and Japanese support for their position and isolating Vietnam helped reinforce group solidarity, even though they constantly had to reconcile differences among themselves on the proper approach to the Kampuchean problem.

ASEAN has also been a useful framework for bargaining for support from friendly countries such as Japan and the United States. From the beginning, the ASEAN concept was attractive and virtually non-controversial in the member countries because it asserted regional associations and gave the appearance of reducing dependence on external powers. Its effectiveness, derived from dealing as a group on behalf of one or more members in economic negotiations with outside countries, has been most evident in negotiations with Japan over limits on its production of artificial rubber (which competed with natural rubber exports from Malaysia, Indonesia, and Thailand) and in seeking modification of Australian civil aviation rules (which discriminated against some ASEAN national airlines, especially Singapore's). Regular official dialogues with Australia, Canada, the European Communities, Japan, New Zealand, and the United States and coordination of positions in international fora have become important ASEAN functions. In addition, ASEAN-wide private-sector organizations, such as the ASEAN Chamber of Commerce and a myriad of more specialized industry associations, have been useful in forging links among businessmen and professionals and between them and the governments.

The existence of ASEAN has contributed in other less tangible ways to the favorable climate in which the members have pursued their development objectives. Prior to the establishment of ASEAN, the member countries were often regarded from the outside as small and constantly bickering, a kind of Southeast Asian "Balkans," an image which Indonesia's "confrontation" campaign against Malaysia, the Philippines's claims to the Malaysian state of Sabah, and the well-publicized separation of Singapore and Malaysia helped to reinforce. The subordination of these previously strong national differences to regional unity has helped to provide a new image of countries working together and to attract foreign investors and traders.

III. THE TRIANGLE: THE UNITED STATES, JAPAN, AND ASEAN

The American and Japanese governments recognize that they have similar overall interests in the ASEAN region, yet they frequently pursue different kinds of policies. The principal differences arise from the historical evolution of U.S. and Japanese postwar policies and their relations with the Southeast Asian region. As a result of cold war rivalry, the United States expanded its worldwide interests and became the paramount military power in the area, whereas Japan's high rate of economic growth and active search for suppliers and markets propelled it into the position of the largest economic partner of the ASEAN group. In the political-security sphere, the United States and Japan play complementary roles, one stressing military presence, the other the economic components of security, both important to the ASEAN governments. In the economic sphere, Americans and Japanese cooperate in some areas, compete in others, and have divergent but nonconflicting interests in still others. For their part, the ASEAN governments recognize differences between the United States and Japan and approach each of them distinctively. As a result, the issues arising in U.S. relations with the ASEAN members are similar in many ways to those arising in Japanese-ASEAN relations, but there are variations.

The Evolution of U.S.-ASEAN Relations

Relations between the United States and the ASEAN countries have changed in some significant respects during the post-World War II period. The United States remains very important to the ASEAN group, but its relative significance to these countries has declined. On the other hand, the economic significance to the United States of the ASEAN countries has tended to increase, but Southeast Asia has become more remote from central issues in U.S. national security policy. In general, governmental relationships are very good. The ASEAN countries are seen by the United States as a model of what developing countries should be like -- non-Communist, trade-oriented, relatively stable politically, and engaged in regional cooperation. The United States is seen by most of the established ASEAN elites as a supportive superpower. Some would like it to be more

active in the region, but others feel that the current
U.S. presence, compared with the Vietnam War era, is
quite comfortable. Where issues do arise, it is
generally at points where U.S. global interests are
not easily compatible with ASEAN regional concerns,
for example, U.S. strategic and commercial interests
in international waterways versus Indonesian and
Philippines interests in drawing territorial sea
boundaries around their entire archipelagos. In such
instances, the ASEAN countries frequently complain of
a lack of American attention to their region and
interests.

In the immediate postwar period, the United
States paid little attention to Southeast Asia other
than the Philippines, which became independent in
1946. However, following the outbreak of Communist
insurgencies in a number of countries in 1948, the
extension of the cold war into East Asia after the
victory by China by Mao Zedong's forces, and the
beginning of the Korean War, Washington regarded the
future ASEAN countries as highly vulnerable to
Communist subversion or aggression. The Vietnam War
heightened the perception in the United States of the
entire Southeast Asian region as a source of security
concerns. Yet United States interests and
responsibilities there were always interpreted
somewhat selectively. The security of the
Philippines, for historical reasons and because of
the U.S. bases there, was regarded as of paramount
importance. Thailand was seen as strategically
important because of its proximity to Vietnam
(Thailand became the site of U.S. air and naval bases
during the Vietnam War) and because it blocked land
access routes to Malaysia and Indonesia. Indonesia,
because of its huge size, location, and resources, was
also considered potentially very important, but, in
contrast to its actions in South Vietnam at the same
time, the United States did not make strenuous efforts
to prevent what in the early 1960s appeared to an
almost a certainty -- the Communist Party's winning
power in Indonesia. The United States, however, did
provide economic and military aid to Indonesia during
the 1950s and even late into the "Confrontation"
period and played a critical role in effecting the
transition of West Irian from Dutch to Indonesian rule
in an effort to win Indonesian favor. Support for
Malaysia and Singapore were regarded as a Commonwealth
responsibility; the relations with Washington of these
two countries, especially the former, were somewhat
distant.

The United States established formal security arrangements with only two Southeast Asian countries, the Philippines and Thailand. Indonesia has always formally maintained a nonaligned foreign policy, and Malaysia and Singapore have also eschewed military alignment with large powers. The bilateral U.S.-Philippine Security Treaty dates from 1951, and the 1954 Manila Pact (which also had established the now dissolved Southeast Asian Treaty Organization) states that the United States and other signatories (including the Philippines and Thailand) will consult and provide aid in accordance with their constitutional processes in the event of an attack in the treaty area. A separate bilateral protocol to the Manila treaty, between the United States and Thailand, dating from 1962 assures the Thais that the United States considers these obligations to be bilateral and not contingent on agreement of other Manila Pact countries.

U.S. foreign-aid levels have reflected the selective nature of U.S. relationships with Southeast Asian countries and the changes over time in the degree of U.S. concern in the region. During the 1953-61 period, United States foreign assistance went mostly to Thailand and the Philippines, which received annual assistance averaging $63.4 million and $55.6 million respectively. In the subsequent years of massive U.S. aid to South Vietnam, assistance to neighboring Southeast Asian countries also increased, especially to Thailand as compensation for the use of base facilities and for Thailand's dispatch of combat soldiers to Vietnam. The annual average level of assistance to Thailand in the 1962-75 period was $102.7 million, two-thirds of it military assistance and more than 90 percent grants rather than concessional loans. Aid to the Philippines in the 1962-75 period also increased to an average $72.4 million annually, but in this case nearly two-thirds was economic aid. Indonesia by the late 1960s had become by far the largest recipient of U.S. aid among the ASEAN countries, representing the U.S. effort to help the New Order consolidate its position. Aid to this country quadrupled from an average annual $30 million in the 1953-61 period to $121.6 million in 1962-75, 90 percent of it economic assistance, especially food. In contrast, Malaysia received less than $14.6 million annually and Singapore but $1.5 million annually between 1962 and 1975.

The present U.S. posture toward ASEAN emerged

30

during the Vietnam War period as the United States sought to disengage itself from what became increasingly regarded in Washington as a gross overcommitment of resources to a South Vietnamese government that was not making an adequate effort to defend itself. In the 1969 Guam Doctrine, President Nixon stated that U.S. allies would bear the primary responsibility for their own defense against subversion, whereas the United States would provide a nuclear umbrella and defense against conventional attack by any large power. The Sino-American rapproachement in the early 1970s and the establishment of relations between China and the ASEAN countries of Malaysia, Thailand, and the Philippines in 1974 and 1975 largely removed the most important basis of U.S. security concern in the Southeast Asia region itself -- that there was a serious threat to the non-Communist governments in the region from China. After the 1975 collapse of the Thieu and Lon Nol governments in South Vietnam and Cambodia respectively, the United States was widely regarded as wanting to reduce its security commitments in the Southeast Asian region. With the withdrawal from Thailand of U.S. military personnel related to the Vietnam War, a U.S. military presence has remained only in the Philippines.

Since the closing years of the Vietnam War, there has been considerable doubt within ASEAN as to whether the United States would intervene militarily to assist an ally in Southeast Asia. The two more likely scenarios concern Thailand and the Philippines, not merely because these are the countries with which the United States has formal treaty obligations, but also because of their apparent security problems. As for Thailand, it seems unlikely that U.S. commitments would be. called upon or that, if they were, U.S. assistance would take the form of direct military intervention. Domestic constraints in both countries would probably prevent a major U.S. military involvement. Moreover, since the Vietnamese occupation of Kampuchea, Bangkok has sought to manage its border situation carefully to avoid conflict with Vietnam, and it has compensated for the uncertainty about future U.S. support by establishing a close relationship with China. Thus major conventional Vietnamese assault across the border seems implausible. As for the Philippines, the most probable reason for U.S. military involvement would be to protect its military bases and citizens in the Philippines from hostile domestic forces rather than

31

because of an external attack on that country. This is conceivable only if a truly revolutionary situation develops in that country.

Although direct U.S. military involvement on behalf of any ASEAN government seems unlikely to be requested or granted, the United States has supported the ASEAN governments in other, more relevant ways in their recent principal security preoccupation -- the problems arising out of the Vietnamese invasion of Kampuchea. One consequence was a flood of new refugees at the Thai-Kampuchean border, adding to the massive numbers of boat refugees leaving Vietnam and landing in Thailand, Malaysia, and Indonesia, especially in 1979 and 1980. The United States took the leadership in organizing an international relief effort to support these refugees and itself has accepted for ultimate asylum half the refugees, who were considered a serious social, economic, and even security problem by the affected ASEAN governments. With some reluctance, because of the atrocities associated with the Pol Pot government in Kampuchea, the United States also voted with the ASEAN countries to maintain this government's seat in the United Nations on the grounds that the new government was imposed by force from the outside and should not be recognized. When Vietnamese troops briefly crossed the Thai border in mid-1980, the United States joined the ASEAN countries in condemning Vietnam and accelerated the delivery of arms shipments to Thailand. After having sharply dropped from the Vietnam War period, levels of U.S. military aid to Thailand increased in the early 1980s, rising from $37.4 million in fiscal year 1980 to $96.2 million in fiscal year 1983.

The United States and ASEAN find themselves in basic agreement on most political and security issues, but there is a continuing fear in ASEAN that U.S. policy is so fixed on other great powers and global political and economic considerations, that it is difficult for smaller countries, even such old friends as the ASEAN governments consider themselves to be, to get proper consideration for their interests. One persisting suspicion in ASEAN, for example, is that the U.S. positions in Kampuchea may have been shaped more by U.S. interest in improving its relations with China than by U.S. attentiveness toward ASEAN. Because of the genuine fear in the ASEAN region of China as a longer-term security threat, a U.S. policy that appears to be building up China's military

32

capabilities, whatever China's intentions may ultimately be, can only be troubling. The U.S. interest in China as well as the United States's own military buildup is seen in some influential quarters in the ASEAN region as reflecting too narrow a focus on the Soviet military threat. The ASEAN governments generally desire the United States to maintain a regional balance of power with the Soviet Union, and they thus appreciate a continuing U.S. naval presence in their region and the maintenance of base facilities in the Philippines, but they also are uncomfortable with the possibility that the United States might focus its attention too heavily on the military competition with the Soviet Union at the expense of its economy and its global economic role, which are very important to ASEAN's continued economic growth.

Indeed, the current ASEAN test of the sincerity of American protestations of keen interest in it relates more to the future of U.S. economic policies than to its military support, the reduced scope of which seems quite well accepted. American perspectives have shifted in the same direction. As military threats to the present order in the ASEAN countries have receded, U.S. policy toward the region has emphasized economic rather than strategic dimensions. At the same time as the U.S. security presence was being reduced, U.S. rhetorical support for the highly promising ASEAN group and its economic interests in the region increased. A U.S.-ASEAN bilateral dialogue was initiated in 1977, and since 1979, the United States secretary of state has joined with his Japanese, Australian, and New Zealand counterparts each year for expanded dialogue with the ASEAN foreign ministers at the conclusion of their foreign ministers meeting. During the later part of the 1970s, economic issues dominated these meetings. The United States found it impossible to accommodate ASEAN's requests for special consideration over and above other developing countries, for example, its proposed STABEX scheme to stabilize the ASEAN countries' export earnings. Moreover, although ASEAN was regarded as a moderate force in the Group of 77 developing countries, the ASEAN countries urged positive U.S. consideration of the Common Fund proposal to stabilize world commodity prices, a proposal that many in the U.S. government thought constituted too much interference with market forces. In recent years, much of the dialogue between the United States and ASEAN in the economic realm has focused on more specific issues involving U.S. trade and investment in the region. As ASEAN countries have joined the ranks of the "middle income" countries and U.S. bilateral economic assistance in the region has declined, foreign-aid issues have become less prominent. Nevertheless, there is general dissatisfaction in ASEAN with what is regarded as decreased U.S. appreciation for the problems of developing countries under the Reagan administration. Despite these differences, U.S. relations with ASEAN have been cordial, and a basic similarity of outlook and interest has existed between the U.S. government and ASEAN governments on the need for a continued active U.S. economic role in the region and the great importance of access to markets and investment capital as elements in the developmental process.

The Evolution of the Japanese-ASEAN Relationship

The ASEAN nations occupy a relatively higher profile in Japanese than in U.S. international economic relations and foreign policy. Economically, they account for a significant share of Japan's trade and overseas investment. It is indicative of the degree of Japanese economic interaction with the ASEAN region that some 37 percent of its foreign assistance in the 1960-1981 period went to these countries, about half of this to Indonesia alone. Japan provides more than 40 percent of all the foreign assistance received by the ASEAN countries. More than a quarter of Japanese government foreign scholarships are given to students from the ASEAN countries. Every recent Japanese prime minister has visited the region, usually soon after taking office. Japan regularly consults the ASEAN countries on regional and global issues and has assumed the position of speaker for ASEAN at the annual economic summit conferences of the seven large industrial nations.

Japan's relations with the ASEAN countries, of course, are still influenced by the legacy of Japanese occupation during the Second World War. At that time Japan occupied for more than three years every country that is now an ASEAN member. The impact of Japanese occupation and the memory of it left are generally unfavorable, but not uniform, in the region. In the Philippines, the occupation delayed the coming of independence, which had already been promised by the United States, and the Japanese treated the local population very cruelly. In Malaya and Singapore, brutal treatment was meted out to the overseas Chinese population. In Indonesia also, the occupation was harsh, and there are bitter memories, but the Japanese encouraged the Indonesian independence movement and provided military training to Indonesian units, which later formed the base of the Republic of Indonesia's army. The Indonesians were able to take advantage of the war to throw off Dutch rule. Thailand was treated as an ally rather than an occupied country.

At the end of the World War, the hopes of Japan's wartime leaders for a Japan-dominated Greater East Asia Co-prosperity Sphere lay completely shattered. So, too, but at first less obviously, did the prewar colonial order in Southeast Asia. The governments of the newly independent states were concerned about the revival of Japanese militarism after the United States began to rehabilitate Japan as an ally. Although most Southeast Asian leaders appreciated the main reason for this change -- to help contain communism in Asia -- some wanted reassurances. The U.S.-Philippines Mutual Security Treaty was designed to make the Philippines confident of protection against Japan as much as, if not more than, against the newly established Communist government in China.

This regional environment and Japan's own internal revulsion after the war toward international political and military involvements led to a low-key postwar approach to the region that emphasized trade and economic cooperation. Only more recently has Japan, still somewhat hesitantly, pursued a more explicitly political or diplomatic role. Initially, Japan's postwar return to the region began in the mid-1950s with reparation agreements. These generally provided credits to the ASEAN countries that could then be used to buy goods in Japan, thus reestablishing Japan's prewar markets. Japan's foreign-aid program was established as a replacement for the reparations agreements and initially focused almost exclusively on the ASEAN region. Japan's early postwar foreign investment activity also emphasized acquisition of raw material resources for Japanese industry, and Southeast Asia was one important source of these resources.

A major expansion of Japan's regional economic role occurred in the late 1960s. In 1966, Japan initiated a series of Ministerial Conferences for the Economic Development of Southeast Asia and it joined the Asia and Pacific Council (ASPAC), an ultimately unsuccessful eight-nation regional association. The

Asian Development Bank, in which Japan became the major donor and appoints the president, opened its doors in December 1966, and, in 1967, Japan became a main contributor to the Inter-Government Group on Indonesia, established to assist the new Indonesian government under President Suharto. Concomitantly with the double-digit growth of the Japanese economy, Japan by the early 1970s had become the first or second largest trading partner of every ASEAN country and was a major factor in the development of the entire region. Despite its efforts to separate economics from politics, inevitably its large economic role had political implications for the ASEAN governments. It meant a growing political stake in the region for Japan as well.

In Southeast Asia the rapid expansion of Japanese economic ties also began to generate a political backlash. There were less severe anti-Japanese riots in Jakarta during Prime Minister Kakuei Tanaka's visit in 1974 and less outbursts in Bangkok. The Japanese government reacted by increasing its aid to the region, cautioning its business community, and looking for a new formula to restore a lower political posture. The new foreign policy formula that evolved under the 1976-78 Fukuda Cabinet emphasized Japan's more general "omnidirectional" foreign policy, its renunciation of a military role in Southeast Asia, and economic assistance to the ASEAN organization. In August 1977, Prime Minister Fukuda was one of the three foreign prime ministers who met with the ASEAN heads of government following their second summit conference in Kuala Lumpur, where he promised $1 billion in aid for ASEAN's proposed large-scale industrial projects. Stopping in Manila on the way home, Fukuda delivered a speech, quickly labeled "The Fukuda Doctrine," spelling out the key points in Japan's future relationship with ASEAN. Japan would encourage peaceful coexistence between ASEAN and the Indochinese countries, Japan would never become a military power and Japan's relationship with ASEAN would be based on "heart to heart" diplomacy.

The emphasis on large-scale projects may have been associated with a particular period in the Japanese-ASEAN relationship when Japanese policy was heavily affected by the Tanaka riots, and highly visible assistance programs were believed needed to counteract bad publicity. In the 1980s, Japan's economic assistance has tended to be lower keyed. Visits by Prime Ministers Suzuki in 1981 and Nakasone in 1983 were accompanied by Japanese offers of economic assistance, but these were smaller in scale and were pragmatically oriented. One important development was Japan's effort to strengthen human resource development in Southeast Asia by establishing training centers providing professional and technical skills.

Following the anti-Tanaka riots, Japan also attempted to strengthen its cultural and educational links with the ASEAN countries. A "youth-ship" program was initiated, and a large Japanese contribution was made to the ASEAN Cultural Fund. Moreover, a private foundation, the Toyota Foundation, became active in cultural exchange programs with the ASEAN countries and has subsidized the translation into Japanese and publication of numerous Southeast Asian books. The government-sponsored Japan Foundation spends about 15 percent of its funds on projects involving ASEAN.

Despite these efforts, however, it is perhaps in the cultural arena that Japan's links with the ASEAN countries remain the weakest. Contacts between Southeast Asian and Japanese elites have been limited. In Southeast Asia and Japan there is probably more elite and public knowledge about the United States and Western Europe than about each other, and, indeed, much of the information about each other is derived from Western sources. One measure of this is the educational preferences of overseas ASEAN students. According to data collected by the Japanese Foreign Ministry, of the 46,108 ASEAN students studying abroad in 1979, only 680 (1.5 percent) were in Japanese institutions. In contrast, 17,258 (37.4 percent) were studying in the European Communities countries (most of these in the United Kingdom), and 16,500 (35.8 percent) were studying in the United States.

People-to-people links with the ASEAN countries, however, are obviously increasing. The number of Japanese Foreign Ministry personnel in embassies in the ASEAN countries (less Brunei) has increased from 94 in 1973 to 165 in 1983 (or from 3.2 percent of all ministry personnel to 4.4 percent). The Japanese business community in the region is estimated to number about 40,000. The number of Japanese visiting the ASEAN region has vastly increased, from about 33,000 in 1970 to more than half a million in 1984.

Moreover, knowledge of Japan in ASEAN is increasing as a by-product of efforts in some ASEAN countries to emulate Japan's success. Before World War II, Japan had been admired by many nationalist movements in Asia for its ability to remain independent, adopt Western technology, and successfully compete with the European powers. In the postwar years, Japan has been seen as a model of rapid economic growth and as the first non-European country to become industrialized. In much of the rest of Asia, politicians and economic planners are seeking inspiration from Japan, as do Americans in the field of management and other areas. Japan is most explicitly held up as a model in Malaysia (the Look East policy) and Singapore (the Learn from Japan policy). Policies to actually adopt Japanese practices have so far been fairly limited -- Singapore is interested in adopting the Japanese "police box" system, and Malaysia has established trading companies and is sending trainees to Japan -- but the possibilities for further growth along these lines are intriguing to many and may reinforce the broader people-to-people contacts promoted by the Japanese government.

The Political-Security Triangle

ASEAN, Japanese, and American security interests and policies coalesce in what amounts to a triangular security relationship. But this relationship is only indirectly acknowledged and rests on a variety of ambiguities. Although these ambiguities contribute to the acceptability of the relationship and make for useful flexibility, they can also be the source of some discomfort. There is latent tension among the continuing U.S. military presence in the region and its desire that Japan assume a broader self-defense role, the ASEAN desire to minimize the involvement of large powers in the security of the region, and the Japanese desire not to become a military power.

The ASEAN governments look to the United States as the ultimate external guarantor of their security. However, most of the ASEAN countries are formally nonaligned, and all, except Brunei, which was not then independent, are signatories of the 1971 Kuala Lumpur Declaration calling for Southeast Asia to become, as noted before, a Zone of Peace, Freedom and Neutrality (ZOPFAN). Among the stated objectives of ASEAN is the eventual elimination of foreign bases from the

38

region. The United States, however, continues to maintain important air and naval installations in the Philippines, and Australian and New Zealand military contingents are in Malaysia and Singapore. These arrangements, despite the ultimate ZOPFAN objective, represent a Western military presence that the ASEAN governments regard as a concrete and welcome manifestation of a continuing security interest and commitment. Similarly, bilateral arrangements between the U.S. and individual ASEAN countries providing for military assistance and training strengthen self-defense capabilities in the region, and other arrangements giving the United States transit rights strengthen ASEAN's entitlement to American support.

Despite the recent upswing in U.S. military aid to the region, the security of the ASEAN countries themselves is relatively low on the agenda of current American security concerns because of the relative stability of the region and the absence of any immediate and pressing external threats to the ASEAN group. However, U.S. security interests in Southeast Asia usually have been defined not primarily with respect to the intrinsic significance of the region, but rather with respect to its role in the global strategic and economic picture. Thus, a main reason for U.S. intervention in Vietnam was the determination of successive American administrations to contain China, then seen as a country bent on dominating East Asia. Today, strategic thinking in U.S. official circles usually sees the ASEAN countries in terms of their geopolitical location commanding vital sea and air links between the Indian Ocean and the South China Sea. These links are seen as more immediately significant to Japan than to the United States. However, the maintenance of a U.S. military presence in Southeast Asia is regarded as essential to American credibility with not just the ASEAN group but also the Northeast Asian countries of Japan and China, and these later, of course, are regarded as of intrinsic strategic value in terms of U.S.-Soviet military competition. After the Soviet Union began to use naval facilities in Vietnam's Cam Ranh Bay, it seemed all the more important that the United States maintain a counterbalancing force in the region to show that it was not abandoning security responsibilities in Southeast Asia. From this broader regional and global perspective, the strategic value of the U.S. presence, especially the bases in the Philippines, has probably continued to increase over the years in the eyes of U.S. policymakers.

Japan also depends on the United States as the ultimate guarantor of its security. Since World War II, Japan has taken an exceptionally narrow view of its security interests. Japan's constitution, written in collaboration with U.S. occupation authorities after the war, is conventionally interpreted in Japan as limiting the nation's military activities strictly to self-defense (and, according to a minority interpretation in Japan, as banning military forces entirely). Increased defense efforts remain a politically sensitive topic in Japan, where the military is remembered for its role in suppressing political parties in the 1930s and leading Japan down a path of aggression toward national self-destruction. Despite some growth of concern about the international security environment and reduced opposition to the U.S.-Japan Security Treaty, there remains strong domestic opposition to a large buildup of Japanese forces and to any kind of external commitment. Thus Japan relies on the United States to complement weaknesses in its own defense posture and to maintain a global and regional balance of power.

Japan has a larger economic stake in the ASEAN region than has the United States. The Strait of Malacca, between Malaysia and Singapore on the north and the Indonesian island of Sumatra on the south, is a strategic waterway for Japan. Through this strait in 1979 passed 78 percent of Japan's crude oil imports, 41 percent of its iron ore imports, 35 percent of its steel exports, 63 percent of its cement exports, and 38 percent of its automobile exports. Thus a U.S. military presence in the region, to the extent that it reinforces stability there and balances other powers, is generally appreciated in Japanese government and business circles.

Reflecting the similarity of ASEAN and Japanese security interests, the Japanese and ASEAN governments all expressed anxiety when the United States, during the early years of the Carter administration, announced its intention to withdraw all its ground troops from South Korea. This was seen in these governments as potentially destabilizing the basic structure of regional security, and their anxieties played a role in the subsequent change in U.S. policy. On the other hand, there are fears in Japan and the ASEAN countries alike that the United States is taking too confrontational a position toward the Soviet Union, provoking a larger Soviet military buildup, and increasing rather than reducing

40

international insecurity. Thus, although the dominant U.S. perception is that the main security threat to the region lies in the Soviet military buildup, in Japan and the ASEAN region there is a tendency to see danger in the interaction of Soviet and American security policies. In particular, loose American talk of a strategic entente among China, Japan, and the United States has caused concern in Japan, where it is regarded as provocative to the Soviet Union, and in ASEAN, where China is regarded with deep distrust.

There is also general agreement between the ASEAN governments and Japan that Japan should not play a military role in the region. U.S. pressure on Japan to assume increased self-defense responsibilities is regarded with some trepidation in the ASEAN region, despite Japan's very cautious approach to increasing its security role and its close and supportive relations with all the ASEAN region. The Fukuda Doctrine, expressing Japan's desire to promote peaceful coexistence between the ASEAN and the Indochinese states, continued a tradition of treading carefully and safely in international politics. Japan would play a constructive political role in the region, but not a military one.

The Japanese government thus finds itself in the difficult position of wanting to appear to its ally, the United States, as increasing its share of defense and international responsibilities but of wanting to minimize the appearance of doing so to the Japanese public. Moreover, Japan does not want to stimulate fears of revived Japanese militarism in other Asian countries, including the ASEAN group. One solution to this dilemma has been the evaluation of the concept of "comprehensive security." First elaborated by a task force for former Prime Minister Ohira in 1979, comprehensive security emphasizes that social and economic development is at least as important to the security of developing countries as military forces. Through its economic aid program, mutually beneficial trade and investment relations, and financial assistance for special problems such as the Indochinese refugee problem, Japan would be making a substantial comprehensive security contribution in the third world. At the same time, Japan's aid program has included enhanced economic assistance to countries deemed strategically important. The only such country within ASEAN is Thailand, which now hosts the largest Japanese embassy in the world outside of the United States, primarily because of aid personnel.

The ASEAN governments have generally expressed support for the comprehensive security concept, stressing that economic assistance is an important ingredient of their efforts toward economic development and "national resilience." It is also recognized that economic assistance can help free ASEAN government budget funds for military spending. However, although the ASEAN countries find the comprehensive security doctrine quite compatible with their views of what Japan's security role should be, they tend to be critical of its implementation. They question how much credit Japan should receive for contributions it would be making anyway for its own economic interest, and they argue that Japan could be doing much more in terms of opening markets, increasing technology transfers, and providing foreign assistance. In some ASEAN countries, especially Indonesia, military and security specialists have expressed an interest in receiving Japanese arms and military technology, arguing that this would help them improve their own defense capabilities and thus provide for regional security, including Japan's. Japan has rejected informal probes of this sort, pointing out that it has been a tenet of Japanese foreign policy not to export military items. And exception, however, has been made on some technology destined for the United States; this has been justified by reference to the principle of mutuality in the alliance relationship.

Comprehensive security is also highly complementary to the U.S. presence in the region. The United States government accepts Japanese domestic constraints and ASEAN fears regarding an overseas Japanese role. Its position is not that Japan should assume military commitments in Southeast Asia but that it should be taking over more of the responsibility for its own conventional military defense to free U.S. resources for global commitments. In theory, therefore, the comprehensive security definition of Japan's security role in Southeast Asia appears satisfactory to all three sides.

One practical problem with Japan's promise not to become a military power in Southeast Asia lies in the ambiguity of the concept of "self-defense." In response to U.S. pressure, Japan recently has made a number of significant commitments to expanding its self-defense missions and capabilities, usually announced on visits by Japanese prime ministers to Washington. These include Prime Minister Suzuki's

42

1981 statement that Japan would undertake to defend sea-lanes stretching 1,000 miles to the south and Prime Minister Nakasone's statements in 1983 that Japan could play a role in closing off strategic straits through the Japanese archipelago to Soviet warships in the event of conflict. Although these commitments were made without any specific new force improvement plans, they were disturbing to some Southeast Asian leaders who feared they portended a large Japanese military presence in their region. In 1982 both President Suharto of Indonesia and President Marcos of the Philippines independently expressed their concern in Washington.

To allay ASEAN fears, Prime Minister Nakasone undertook a trip to the region in April and May of 1983. He assured Southeast Asian leaders that Japan's military buildup was completely defensive in nature and that the 1,000 miles of sea-lane would not encroach upon Southeast Asian waters. (In Japanese planning, these sea-lanes begin near Tokyo and Osaka and terminate in the ocean east of Taiwan, still far from the Philippines; Nakasone and Marcos reportedly poured over maps indicating the Japanese view of the sea-lanes.) The emphasis of this trip was on "personal diplomacy," and, in this respect, the trip appears to have been quite successful. However, resentments against Japan are not far underneath the surface and can quickly reemerge in the event of additional Japanese defense measures.

Even though Japan's expenditure of one percent of GNP on defense appears small to Americans, who spend 6 percent of their GNP on defense, Japan has built up a defense establishment that by all measures except manpower is larger than that of the ASEAN countries together. The ASEAN countries regard U.S.-Japan security relations, therefore, as an important check on an independent and potentially much larger and more threatening Japanese security policy. In the absence of the security treaty and a friendly and effective U.S. presence in the region, the rationale for Japanese rearmament would be greatly strengthened. On the other hand, the U.S.-Japan relationship becomes a source of concern when it appears that the United States is contemplating making Japan its surrogate in Asia or is encouraging Japan to move into a more extensive security role.

The Economic Triangle

The major external economic partners of the ASEAN countries are the United States and Japan. These two countries alone in 1982 purchased 43.6 percent of ASEAN's exports (28.8 percent by Japan, 14.8 percent by the United States) and provided 36.5 percent of ASEAN's imports (22 percent from Japan, 14.5 percent from the United States). In contrast, intra-ASEAN trade has remained at about a 15 percent level, and only about 2 percent of ASEAN trade has been with socialist countries. Although figures for foreign investment are much more elusive and difficult to compare, by the end of 1980, Japan and the United States accounted for an estimated 44 percent of the direct foreign investment in the then five ASEAN countries (29 percent by Japanese investors and 15 percent by American).

The economic significance of Japan and the United States to ASEAN, however, derives not simply from trade and investment, but also from their influence on the global trading environment and the importance to ASEAN of their relationship with each other. The continued success of ASEAN development strategies depends on expansion of exports, which in turn depends on the healthy growth of the major economies and the maintenance of an open trading system. Japan's high economic growth during the 1960s and into the 1970s was a major factor behind the expansion of ASEAN's exports of primary products in the same period. The United States has been a primary market for ASEAN's growing export of manufactured products, and its recent high growth rate has helped improve ASEAN's growth performance after the world recession of the early 1980s.

Trade. The highly complementary nature of Japan's economy with the ASEAN economies as they are presently structured makes the trading relationship important to them both. (See figure 1.) Japan looks to ASEAN for strategic raw materials and a market for its industrial exports. ASEAN depends on Japan as a prime market for its exports of crude petroleum, fuels, raw materials, and agricultural products. In 1979-80, for example, almost 57 percent of ASEAN mineral fuel exports and almost 42 percent of ASEAN's other raw material exports went to Japan; Japan has taken all of Indonesia's liquified natural gas (LNG) and is the principal market for Indonesian, Malaysian, and Brunei oil. These petroleum exports have resulted

44

Figure 1:
ASEAN, Japan and the U.S.—
The Trade Triangle: 1982

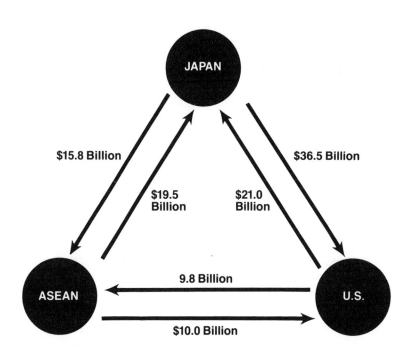

Source: IMF "Direction of Trade" Statistics

in a large trade surplus with Japan for ASEAN as a whole (about $4.5 billion in a two-way trade of $34.5 billion in 1982), but Singapore and Thailand have persistent trade deficits with Japan. All the ASEAN countries, including those with trade surpluses, voice complaints about the lack of access for their manufactured products. Although the share of primary products in ASEAN's total exports has fallen below 70 percent, they still represent 90 percent of Japan's total purchases. The pattern of their primary products for Japan's manufactured goods trade is widely regarded in ASEAN as an unsatisfactory, "colonial" relationship, and increasingly it is a bone of contention.

The United States is the principal market for ASEAN's manufactured goods, which now account for almost a third of U.S. imports from the ASEAN region. About four-fifths of U.S. exports to ASEAN also are manufactured products, half consisting of machinery and transportation equipment. Like Japan, the United States has had a trade surplus with Singapore (an entrepot center through which U.S. manufactured goods are marketed) and a large deficit with Indonesia. However, because the United States imports much less petroleum from the region, its overall trade relationships has been more balanced than Japan's. In 1982, the United States exported almost $10 billion to the region and imported a little more than $10 billion, amounting to a tenfold increased since 1970.

Only the Philippines buys a higher percentage of its imports from the United States than from Japan. Because of increased oil imports from the Middle East to Thailand and the Philippines and the growth of sales to ASEAN by the newly industralizing economies such as South Korea and Taiwan, the shares of both Japan and the United States in the ASEAN import markets have decreased over the past decade. However, the United States has succeeded better than Japan in maintaining its ASEAN market share. The U.S. share between 1972 and 1982 dropped slightly from 15.4 percent to 14.5 percent, while the Japanese share of ASEAN markets declined from 26.6 percent to 22.0 percent.

ASEAN, of course, figures much less significantly in the economies of its large partners than Japan and the United States do in the ASEAN economies. The ASEAN countries as a group are the fourth largest trading partner of the United States (after Canada,

Japan, and the European Communities group). However, U.S. imports from ASEAN in 1982 represented only 4.6 percent of the U.S. total, and sales to ASEAN were also 4.6 percent of total U.S. exports. These figures, however, represent very substantial gains over the past decade; ten years earlier, ASEAN accounted for 2.6 percent of U.S. imports and 2.7 percent of its exports. In Japan's case, ASEAN is a distant second largest trading partner after the United States, and Indonesia alone in 1982 was Japan's third largest single-country partner after the United States and Saudi Arabia. As a group, ASEAN provided 14.8 percent of Japan's imports (compared with the 18.3 percent provided by the United States) and purchased 10.8 percent of Japan's exports (compared with 26.2 percent for the United States and 12.3 percent for the European Economic Community). ASEAN's higher economic profile with Japan than with the United States, especially its role as a reliable petroleum supplier, gives it more bargaining leverage with Japan and is reflected in the much larger size of Japan's foreign aid to the region.

Investment. As it does in trade with ASEAN, Japan outstrips all other countries in direct foreign investment, with almost $11 billion dollars by 1984, as compared with approximately $8 billion for the United States. This investment has been expanding very rapidly, representing a fourfold increase over 1976. Moreover, ASEAN figures prominently in Japan's total share of foreign investment, taking about one-fifth of the total. After the United States, the largest recipient of Japanese direct foreign investment is Indonesia, where this investment is concentrated in the production and processing of raw materials (especially petroleum, but also aluminum and wood). Although Japan's investments have reflected its raw material needs, Japanese have also invested in manufacturing to improve access to local markets and reduce wage costs in labor-intensive industries. In Thailand, for example, most of Japan's foreign investment is concentrated in small-scale manufacturing in joint ventures with Thai partners.

Japan is the largest foreign investor in Indonesia, Malaysia, and Thailand, whereas the United States is the major investor in the Philippines and Singapore. Much of the U.S. investment in the ASEAN countries has been in the energy sector, accounting for about 74 percent of total U.S. investment in Indonesia in 1977 and 32.6 percent in the

47

Philippines. American direct private investment in ASEAN has been increasing at the rate of 10 to 15 percent annually. This investment constitutes only 2.8 percent of total U.S. world investment, but it is a more substantial 11.3 percent of American investment in the third world. U.S. business representatives with long experience in the region believe that U.S. business interest in the ASEAN has been rapidly growing.

Financial Relations. As in the case of most developing countries, nonconcessional borrowing became an important source of capital for the ASEAN countries. This borrowing was encouraged by the need to finance development, the added costs of importing oil for the Philippines and Thailand, and the relatively low cost of money during the 1970s. The prolonged recession following the second oil crisis of 1979 reduced the ASEAN countries' export earnings and their ability to service their debts. At the same time, the high interest rates, of course, also increased the costs to ASEAN governments and to private companies in these countries of raising new capital and rolling over existing debts. Moreover, as bankers became more cautious, lending conditions generally tightened. By 1981 the average real interest rates on new borrowings for the ASEAN countries had doubled over those of 1970, whereas average grace and maturity periods had decreased greatly. An increasing number of loans were shorter term and at variable rather than fixed rates. These factors, plus the need to finance even a reduced rate of growth through the recession of the early 1980s, resulted in substantially larger debt burdens. Moreover, the high U.S. interest rates have been attracting foreign capital into the U.S. which might otherwise have gone to the ASEAN and other developing countries, and, combined with other factors such as the desire to place capital in a "safe haven," have also pulled out some local capital. It should be noted, however, that, although Indonesia, Malaysia, and Thailand are the world's sixth, eleventh, and fourteenth largest debtors, their short-term debts are not excessive and debt-service ratios have been well below the 20 percent of exports level. Their governments have pursued cautious fiscal policies and made major cuts in their developmental or other spending to meet their external debts. Only the Philippines has been a major exception, its debt-service indicators being nearly the equivalent of Latin American levels.

48

Although except for the Philippines, there is no debt "crisis" in the ASEAN region, the longer-term ability of the ASEAN countries to service their existing debt and prudently expand borrowings again for development purposes depends very much on the macroeconomic policies of the United State and Japan. The rate of growth of these countries, as ASEAN's primary trade partners, has a very important effect on ASEAN's foreign exchange earnings. The other major variable is the interest rate, which could be reduced if the United States were able to reduce its budget deficit. ASEAN is also hoping for greater access to Japan's capital markets. The gradual deregulation and internationalization of these capital markets, under internal as well as U.S. pressure, should result in additional opportunities for the ASEAN countries to raise nonconcessional funds in Japan.

Triangular Economic Relationships. There is a general coincidence of interests between the United States and ASEAN in seeking a liberalization of the Japanese market and a general coincidence of interests between Japan and ASEAN in encouraging the U.S. to resist protectionist sentiments. Nevertheless, because of differences in levels of development, these interests are rarely perceived as similar by the two sides involved and are therefore not actively pursued in a coordinated manner. Although ASEAN stands to gain from U.S. pressure on Japan to open markets for manufactured goods, it often seems to the ASEAN governments that recent Japanese trade concessions have tended to be product-specific rather than systemic and have favored products from the developed countries, thus leaving less scope and political capital for trade concessions to ASEAN. Although the Japanese government and business communities have urged the ASEAN countries to lobby the United States administration to fight protectionism, the Japanese are concerned about automobiles and steel, whereas ASEAN is more worried about textiles and apparel. Moreover, there is a tendency in ASEAN to see Japan's appeals as a diversion from a more real and immediate protectionist problem -- the lack of access for ASEAN manufactures in Japan itself.

From an ASEAN perspective, Japan and the United States are two economic giants whose domestic economic policies and whose economic relations with each other are tremendously important to ASEAN, but virtually beyond ASEAN's ability to influence. On the one hand, there are fears within the ASEAN region that too close economic collaboration between the United States and Japan could reduce consideration of the impact on third countries, limiting ASEAN maneuverability and raising the prospect of economic domination. The predilection of Japan and the United States to resolve economic disputes, whether in the trade or the financial fields, through bilateral negotiations and agreements reinforces these fears. On the other hand, there is also anxiety in the ASEAN region about high levels of tension in the U.S.-Japan economic relationship. If not ameliorated, such trade tensions could strengthen forces of protectionism and economic nationalism in both countries and reduce their ability to work effectively toward maintaining an open world trading system. The ASEAN countries would also suffer if economic frictions affected the political-security relationship between Japan and the United States and generally increased tensions in the broader Pacific Basin region. Basically, the ASEAN governments prefer a competitive, but not antagonistic, U.S.-Japan relationship, with each larger country actively competing for ASEAN affections.

Their economic weakness, compared with Japan and the United States, is inevitably a source of frustration for the ASEAN governments. Especially in difficult times when global markets are contracting and the prices of ASEAN's main commodity exports are falling, ASEAN grievances tend to focus on Japan and the United State because of their importance to the ASEAN region and their influence on the more general global economy. In the case of Japan, the impact of ASEAN grievances on the overall relationship with Japan is sharpened by the saliency of Japan's regional economic role and the relative weakness of other ties in the Japan-ASEAN relationship. In contrast, the impact of economic difficulties with the United States is cushioned by the depth, variety, and importance to the ASEAN countries of their political, economic, and cultural relations with the United States.

IV. CURRENT AND FUTURE ISSUES

Although relationships among the American, Japanese, and ASEAN governments remain highly cooperative, there are areas in which issues are likely to persist or emerge. This chapter will examine more closely seven such areas.

Trade Protectionism

There have been relatively few enduring trade disputes between ASEAN and either the United States or Japan because of the highly complementary nature of ASEAN's trade with the two larger economies. U.S. sales of surplus tin from the strategic stockpile have periodically caused protests from Malaysia and, to a lesser extent, Indonesia and Thailand because the extra supplies on the market drive down the price enjoyed by these tin-producing countries. Another enduring trade issue has been the persistent Japanese balance of payment surplus with Thailand, despite efforts by the Japanese private sector and government to encourage imports from Thailand by setting annual import targets. In the future it is likely that trade issues will become more contentious for several reasons. Because current growth strategies of the ASEAN countries are so highly dependent upon access to overseas markets, obstacles to entry into the U.S. and Japanese markets will be a source of increased concern to the ASEAN governments and exporters. At the same time, ASEAN is exporting more manufactured goods, such as textiles and apparel, which compete with higher-wage U.S. and Japanese industries, and these industries are increasingly anxious to limit the access of ASEAN and other foreign competitors.

Market access issues between Japan and ASEAN manifest themselves in quite different ways from those between the United States and ASEAN. In the case of Japan, ASEAN often is seeking market access for manufactured products. On the other hand, in the U.S. case, the ASEAN countries already enjoy considerable access but are worried that protectionism will restrict the future growth of their exports. In both cases, the ASEAN countries are also concerned about potential non-ASEAN competition, notably from China and Latin America.

51

To ASEAN countries' complaints that Japan imports almost exclusively their raw materials and little in the way of manufactured products, the Japanese respond that, because Japan itself has virtually no raw materials, the Japan-ASEAN pattern of trade is normal for a resource-poor country vis-a-vis resource-rich countries. In other words, the trade patterns are structural in character, not a consequence of protectionist Japanese trade policies. ASEAN trade officials, however, note that Japanese tariffs on some processed or manufactured items are far higher than for raw materials and that joint venture agreements between Japanese and ASEAN partners frequently prohibit or restrict exports back to Japan or to third countries by the ASEAN partner. There also are complaints that Japanese company groups have arrangements to buy among themselves, excluding imports, and that, when Japan does make trade concessions, it does so mainly in response to the United States and Western Europe. In sum, many in the ASEAN region believe Japan is trying to preserve an existing, neo-colonial trading pattern rather than adjusting to the development of cheaper, higher-quality manufacturing in the rest of Asia. In their view, Japan's worldwide trade surplus and its presumed special interest in ASEAN justify special trade efforts on behalf of ASEAN products, especially manufactured goods.

Most of the protectionist sentiment in the United States so far threatens the entry of products from Japan and the newly industrializing countries far more than those of ASEAN. One area in which ASEAN has been affected, however, is in textile and apparel exports. The U.S. textile and garment manufacturing interests argue that their workers are in a similar position to those in developing countries and that protection is needed to prevent further unemployment and raise productivity. Protection in the form of import quotas has long been provided to the industry, and these have gradually been extended to more categories of imports and more countries. In what appeared to be a preelection move in the summer of 1984, the Reagan administration sought to tighten country-of-origin rules to prevent garments manufactured in several countries from being finally exported to the United States from the country with the most room in its U.S. quota, even if only a very small part of the manufacturing were done in that country. Although the ASEAN countries are relatively small exporters to the United States, their exports are growing very rapidly in some cases (for example, in the first five months of 1984, Thailand's garment shipments rose by 97 percent and Indonesia's by 227 percent), and the proposed new country-of origin rules threatened to curtail some of this growth.

The United States also has trade grievances against the ASEAN countries. One issue that is likely to grow in importance involves "intellectual property," that is, the protection of patents, designs, musical recordings, computer software, and the like. For example, Singapore is alleged to be lax on counterfeiters, who attach an American trademark to their products without acquiring the right to do so or who simply copy without respecting the patent or copyright. The growing attention to this issue has been shown in congressional insistence that a country's respect for intellectual property be considered in future grants of tariff preferences (GSP) applied to some products of developing countries.

Some U.S. and Japanese trade officials and businessmen believe that trade issues can be resolved by more active use of the General Agreement on Trade and Tariffs (GATT). They encourage the ASEAN countries to take a more positive attitude to developing new international trading rules, pointing out that this too would help alleviate protectionist pressures in the developed countries. Many trade specialists in the ASEAN group, however, believe that the rules appropriate to the developed countries would, if they agreed to them, leave them forever "hewers of wood and drawers of water" for Japan, the United States, and Western Europe. They argue that export subsidies or trade protection may be needed to allow infant industries in the ASEAN countries to advance against international competition. They point out that both the United States and Japan had quite protectionist trade policies at the equivalent stages in their own economic development.

Another issue is the degree to which Japan and the United States should give special or preferential consideration to ASEAN as a friendly region of rapidly developing market economies. The most concrete suggestion for special consideration came up in the later part of the 1970s, when the ASEAN countries asked their ASEAN dialogue partners to participate in a STABEX system under which these partners would make up for the loss of export earnings should the prices of ASEAN's primary products fall. The ASEAN countries felt such a scheme was justified because many African countries were covered by a similar arrangement with the European Economic Community. Suggestions also have been made, less formally, for special preferences for ASEAN products. The United States position has been that as a global power its policy is to treat all developing countries similarly. However, when the United States provided preferential trade treatment for Caribbean countries under the Reagan administration's Caribbean Basin Initiative, it seemed to ASEAN observers that U.S. policy was inconsistent and accorded ASEAN second-class treatment. The Caribbean exception to general U.S. policy may lead to renewed ASEAN pressures for equal treatment.

Japan has taken a similar position on the need for global trade policies. However, in 1977 the Japanese government agreed to examine the STABEX proposal, and, eventually, it concluded that a STABEX scheme would be of little utility to ASEAN. Although the ASEAN countries have not persisted in pressing this proposal, they tend to expect special attention from Japan as an Asian country, and Japan continues to try to accommodate this expectation through large foreign assistance programs, expanded consultations, and support for the ASEAN organization, without establishing a regional trade preferences scheme. The ASEAN countries individually can also be expected to press Japan harder on questions of market access for manufactured goods and to take measures, such as Indonesia's restrictions on log exports, designed to shift processing and manufacturing from Japan to their own countries.

Foreign Investment

All the ASEAN governments maintain some kind of incentives, including tax holidays and accelerated depreciation, to attract foreign investment. This does not mean, however, that they welcome foreign investors with no strings attached. These governments have a complex set of objectives and political imperatives, which often conflict with the predominant profit and market share maximization motives of the investors. The ASEAN governments are trying to increase employment and the flow of technology, and they may establish performance requirements for training or employment of host country nationals, exporting, or local subcontracting. Foreign companies could be required to observe ethnic guidelines in

54

selecting joint-venture partners or in hiring. In some sectors of the ASEAN economies, foreign participation could be limited, for example, to "production sharing" in the case of Indonesian petroleum. Moreover, foreign investment rules could change because of political considerations or a reassessment of benefits and costs by the host countries; for example, Indonesia recently decided to abolish tax holidays for foreign investors because of revenue losses.

The often high profile of foreign investments and the complex regulations affecting them can create a host of specific problems. Smaller-scale or inefficient competitors can be run out of business. To cite an example, Japanese investment in Indonesia prior to 1974 tended to be small scale and competitive with the local textile industry. Foreign investors can be slow to hire local personnel for higher management positions. Management techniques can be introduced that clash with local business practices. The ASEAN partners in joint ventures can be members of the rich, overseas Chinese minorities or cronies of a president or prime minister, thus appearing to further enrich and strengthen the already wealthy and powerful. Because some foreign investment also is motivated by the desire to escape pollution or safety requirements at home, the same problems are transferred to Southeast Asia, where safeguards are less strict and enforcement lax.

Foreign investment might also not live up to the high expectations of the ASEAN governments. Japanese direct foreign investment has been estimated to have created over 50,00 jobs in each ASEAN country, in most cases only a very tiny fraction of the labor force (e.g., less than a quarter of one percent in the case of Thailand). Technology transfer is another easy source of resentment; if the foreign company is transferring sophisticated technology, it can be charged with failing to offer "appropriate" technology; if it is not using the latest technology, it can be accused of holding back.

The governments of the ASEAN countries and the foreign investors both have an incentive to increase foreign investment, even if neither side achieves its maximum goals with respect to economic development and income distribution or profits. Both parties also recognize that foreign investment is potentially a nationalistic issue that opposition groups can use with effect against the ruling establishments. The 1974 riots at the time of Japanese Prime Minister Tanaka's ASEAN visits are illustrative of the way in which general frustrations arising out of the modernization process combined with local political rivalries can crystallize into resentment against foreign businesses and the host governments that invited them. (Although Japanese foreign investment was only one of a complex set of issues that led to the riots, the fact that the Indonesian government subsequently adopted new measures to expand sectors prohibited to foreign investors, increase the use of the local materials, and require training of Indonesians for management positions reflected the government's recognition of the legitimacy of the some of the complaints and their political potency.) Foreign investors and their local hosts or partners are ready targets because critics argue that the continuation in power of corrupt governments, income inequities, and a variety of other problems are directly related to the way in which foreign capital influences the host society, a more general issue addressed in the next section.

Nationalism and the Development Debate

Outward-looking, export-led development strate-gies are currently being pursued by all the ASEAN governments, increasing their dependency on Japan and the United States. As a result, if export-led development falters -- whether because of the growth of protectionism in the United States, the lack of market access in Japan, slow growth in both countries, an international financial crisis, or some other external reason -- it is likely that many in the ASEAN countries would assign the blame to lack of leadership on the part of the United States and Japan as the two most influential developed countries. Moreover, the developmental process and its inherent problems and stresses are associated with Japan and the United States in the minds of some Southeast Asians. Therefore, export-led development strategies strengthen linkages among Japan, the United States, and ASEAN, but, by the same token, could generate nationalist pressures in favor of limiting these stressful aspects of these external connections.

In recent years, the expression of nationalism in the ASEAN countries has been relatively subdued. However, within the ASEAN government bureaucracies and among the political elites, there are many who chafe at the high degree of dependence on foreign sources of capital and trade despite the obvious benefits. Public expressions of nationalism by ASEAN governmental leaders, however, have tended so far to be directed against smaller developed countries; for example, Britain has been the chief object of much recent Malaysian criticism over a variety of economic issues, and Australia has been criticized by Singapore, Indonesia, and other ASEAN countries over such issues as civil aviation, Australian sentiment for East Timor independence, and Australia's Kampuchean position. ASEAN government criticism of Japan and the United States tends to be expressed more cautiously, probably because it is an issue that can easily be coopted by domestic opposition groups, but it does surface from time to time on such specific issues as U.S. sales of tin from its stockpiles, Japanese tariff policies, and Japan's defense policy.

Outside the governments, economic nationalism comes from many sources, especially from critics within the intellectual and student communities who argue that export-led development reinforces neocolonial and capitalist patterns of exploitation. These critics readily associate foreign economic dominance with domestic problems of social injustice, political repression, and ecological degradation and argue that the economic relationships between their countries and the industrialized world must be altered drastically if true development is to be achieved. In general, however, such arguments are less frequently and less influentially expressed in the ASEAN region than in much of the rest of the developing world. Nevertheless, they represent an alternative perspective that at least lingers and, in some respects, has picked up strength from religious sentiments that denounce the consumerism and materialism associated with Western development strategies (e.g., by Islamic groups in Indonesia and Malaysia) or from broader opposition currents (as in the Philippines). Other sources of economic nationalism come from private entrepreneurs directly disadvantaged by the foreign economic presence and groups that have been dislocated by the development process or indirectly disadvantaged.

The nationalist reaction to foreign economic presence is closely linked with the trade and investment issues just discussed. The potential for more assertive forms of economic nationalism across a broad range of issues appears strongest in the

Philippines and Indonesia. In both, the foreign presence is very visible; in Indonesia it is most prominent in resource exploitation, and, in the Philippines, the economic presence is reinforced by a large foreign military presence. Moreover, in both Indonesia and the Philippines, there is more actual or latent discontent with current leadership, which is expressed most safely by criticizing relationships with foreign business.

Japan's Role in the Security of the ASEAN Region

As discussed in the previous chapter, Japan has defined a security role in the ASEAN region based on pledges that (1) Japan will not be a military power in the region, (2) Japan will not transfer arms or military technology to the region, and (3) Japan will contribute to "comprehensive security" in the region by aiding the economic development of the ASEAN countries through aid, trade, and investment and by financially helping them manage special problems such as the massive refugee flows from Indochina. Although some ASEAN governments would like arms transfers and military assistance from Japan, this Japanese position seems acceptable throughout the region. As part of a long-term process, however, Japan is also strengthening its own national defense efforts, including sea-lane protection toward the south, and, as it does so, fears of a Japanese military role continue to be evoked from time to time.

A question arises why Japan's potential military role creates controversy whereas the continuing American presence or the nearby Chinese presence seems to be of less overt concern. One important consideration is that, for the current generation of ASEAN leaders, men such as Ferdinand Marcos or Suharto, the Japanese military occupation of their countries during the war remains a vivid memory, and, despite all the Japanese assurances to the contrary, they believe it not impossible that it could be repeated. In contrast, although China is also a matter of concern to them because it has provided support to ASEAN Communist parties and has sought to manipulate overseas Chinese communities, it has never militarily occupied any ASEAN country. In addition, the United States and China have maintained their present security roles for a long time, whereas the Japanese role is prospective. A final explanation might be that, because Southeast Asian leaders are on

the defensive regarding the large Japanese economic
presence in their countries, a loud protest against
putative Japanese military activities demonstrates
their independence and willingness to defend national
interests against Japan.

Even increased Japanese self-defense capabilities
involving no direct military role in Southeast Asia
create some uneasiness in ASEAN circles. Some argue
that adding to military capabilities on the Western
side of the ledger could provoke the Soviets into
responding in kind, thus increasing large-power forces
in the wider region, increasing tensions, and
complicating the regional balance. Increased Japanese
capabilities also would allow the United States to
divert forces from the defense of Japan to areas to
the south, and thus might increase the U.S. presence
in the Southeast Asian region and the possibility that
U.S. and Soviet forces might clash. Finally, to the
extent that Japan itself did develop a capacity to
project military power southward, this alone would add
tremendously to its already powerful economic
presence, thus jeopardizing still further the real
independence of the ASEAN countries.

As the U.S. and Japanese governments continue to
fashion a division of labor involving increased
Japanese defense responsibilities, Japan's role
undoubtedly will remain a controversial and sensitive
issue in the ASEAN region.

Kampuchea

Since the Vietnamese invasion of Kampuchea, the
United States and Japan have consistently supported
ASEAN's positions on Kampuchea. Both countries,
however, had some initial concerns that remain,
although in muted fashion. The United States,
following an internal battle within the State
Department, agreed to support ASEAN's struggle to
retain the seat of the Democratic Republic of
Kampuchea (the Khmer Rouge government) in the United
Nations. Those opposed to this position found it
distasteful that the United States should in any way
be appearing to endorse this brutal regime, which had
been responsible for so much killing in Kampuchea
during its almost four years of rule. Japan had hoped
to be a bridge between Vietnam and ASEAN prior to the
Vietnamese invasion of Kampuchea and, to be more
credible in this role, had tried to strengthen its

contacts with Vietnam by providing economic assistance. Because of vigorous ASEAN lobbying after the invasion, Japan, after some hesitation, cut off its aid and condemned Vietnam. Nevertheless, there remains sentiment within Japanese professional diplomatic circles for a resumption of an aid relationship with Vietnam in the interests of promoting peaceful coexistence between Vietnam and the ASEAN countries.

In order to strengthen support for the resistance forces in Kampuchea, the ASEAN governments (especially Singapore and Thailand) made vigorous efforts to bring the two non-Communist factions into a coalition government which the Khmer Rouge. Son Sann became titular leader of the new government, established in 1982, but the coalition government exists, if at all, only on paper. The United States supported the creation of the coalition government and offered nonmilitary assistance to the non-Communist factions once the coalition had been achieved.

A question for U.S. diplomacy is whether U.S. assistance to these groups should be expanded to include weapons. Son Sann, in particular, has lobbied in Washington for military aid and equipment, and his requests have been strongly supported by some of the ASEAN governments. ASEAN as a whole urged arms support for the Kampuchean resistance at the 1984 expanded foreign ministers' meeting. At that meeting they were told by Secretary Schulz that "We will continue to do our part, including moral, political, and humanitarian support for the organizations led by Prince Sihanouk and Son Sann. We will give no support to the Khmer Rouge, whose atrocities outraged the world."

Those Americans who favor providing arms assistance argue that it would help the overall Khmer resistance effort against the Vietnamese and strengthen the non-Communist opposition as opposed to the Khmer Rouge forces, which are well-supplied by Beijing. Those opposing arms aid say that it would put the United States back into a position of military involvement in Indochina, and that, in any case, the limited amount of military supplies needed by Son Sann and Prince Sihanouk can be provided by the ASEAN governments themselves and therefore the only purpose of the request is to engage the United States more deeply in the conflict. So far the latter view has prevailed formally within the Reagan administration, but because of the ASEAN lobbying, the United States is reported to be considering increasing its small financial contributions, first begun in 1982, some of which would go to ASEAN governments for "humanitarian purposes" but could be used by them to free up other monies within their own budgets for arms aid.

A broader question relates to what possible role the United States or Japan could play in facilitating a political solution to the struggle in Kampuchea. During the past five years, the United States has been largely content to support ASEAN's line diplomatically and politically. A more activist U.S. role is inhibited by the priority the U.S. places on good relations with China, which opposes any compromise on the issue, and by the lack of diplomatic relations with Vietnam, a legacy of the Vietnam War period and more recent international political considerations. Perhaps of more importance, however, is that the status quo in Kampuchea does not threaten U.S. interests; thus there is little incentive for it to venture further into an extremely complicated situation, where the main protagonists show few signs of flexibility.

Japan has made several initiatives with respect to Kampuchea; for example, a proposal of an international conference in 1979 and a blueprint for a solution in Kampuchea in 1981 -- all proposed at the meetings the ASEAN foreign ministers hold annually with their Japanese, American, Australian, and some other counterparts and thus clearly associated with ASEAN positions. Aspiration to restore the aid relationship with Vietnam remains, but any genuflection in that direction inevitably attracts ASEAN opposition. In May 1983, Japanese Foreign Minister Abe proposed to his Thai counterpart that Japan increase its aid to Laos (then only $3 million), but even this proposal was rejected by ASEAN on the grounds that it might indirectly help Vietnamese activities in Kampuchea. Japan probably has more interest than the United States in finding a diplomatic solution, but it is unwilling to take the risk of offending the ASEAN nations.

At the present, there seems to be very little prospect for an early solution to the Kampuchean stalemate. The ASEAN strategy of withholding recognition of the Vietnamese-backed Heng Samrin government and of supporting the non-Communist resistance factions while China provides military aid to the Khmer Rouge shows no signs of dislodging the Vietnamese. Indeed the resistance movements have been fighting each other. On the other hand, the Vietnamese have been able neither to suppress opposition within Kampuchea nor to win much diplomatic support for the Heng Samrin government in the face of ASEAN's opposition. The struggle, however, remains highly dependent on Chinese support for the Khmer Rouge and on Soviet support for the Vietnamese and probably will be resolved only as part of an accommodation by these two large Communist powers.

The Philippines

The deteriorating economic and political situation in the Philippines is another major challenge facing both the United States and Japan. U.S. interest lies in its historical relationship with the Philippines, its large military bases, its economic ties, and its human rights concerns. For Japan, the Philippines is its closest Southeast Asian neighbor and a country where Japan also has major economic and even political investments. A collapse of the Philippines into complete chaos or the emergence of new leadership hostile to relations with Japan and the United States would have significant implications for both countries.

The most critical immediate issue for both governments is the extent to which they should support or dissociate themselves from the current Philippine government. In U.S. debate on the subject, the analogy with U.S. support for the late Shah of Iran is often noted; it has been elaborated in a lengthy analysis by a former U.S. ambassador to the Philippines and was even raised in the foreign policy debate of the two presidential candidates in 1984. Marcos continues to display remarkable political resiliency in the face of the mounting political and economic crisis and persistent rumors that he is seriously ill. There is no consensus among observers in either the Japanese or the American governments that the Marcos government will soon disappear. However, it is feared that, if Marcos were to disappear from the scene in the immediate future, a leadership vacuum would result. The prospect of chaos or a cruder form of military authoritarianism, neither desirable in themselves and both of which might hasten the development of a genuine revolutionary situation, also increases U.S. and Japanese reluctance to

62

distance themselves from Marcos.

Under the Carter administration, there was some sharp criticism of human rights violations in the Philippines. During the Reagan administration this criticism was softened to the point that the vice president once even praised Philippine democracy. After the assassination of Benigno Aquino, however, U.S. policy became more nuanced, more responsive to the general crisis crystallized by the assassination. The new emphasis in U.S. policy has been to encourage local forces seeking to modify Marcos's arbitrary rule and, in the long run, to promote liberal democratic institutions equivalent to those prevailing before martial law. Signals that the United States did not unconditionally approve of the Marcos government were combined with measures designed to promote stability and peaceful transition to more democratic institutions. For instance, the U.S. administration rushed aid appropriated for fiscal year 1984 slightly ahead of schedule to ease the beleaguered Philippine economy, but, at the same time, it canceled Reagan's planned visit to the Philippines and other Southeast Asian countries. In September 1983, the United States voted against a $150 million World Bank agricultural loan to the Philippines, but it was clear the loan would nonetheless be approved. Advocates in the U.S. Congress of a more circumspect policy toward the Philippines have sought to reduce foreign assistance or shift some of the military aid to economic aid, to prod Marcos in a more liberal direction. Support for such measures is limited, however, because the Philippine aid budget is so closely tied with the bases agreement, and, in any case, threats of changes seem to have little apparent effect on Marcos. Congress made no cuts in the fiscal year 1985 aid program but shifted half of the $30 million allocated for foreign military sales to economic supporting assistance, a change that is more symbolic than real.

The economic crisis of the Philippines complicates these questions but also gives the United States and Japan some opportunities for leverage. The dependence of the Philippines on its creditors, including these countries and the International Monetary Fund (IMF), gives the creditors an opportunity to compel the government to undertake economic reforms. For the U.S. and Japanese governments it is a question of finding an optimal package of corrective measures that will restore solvency and promote long-term structural adjustments in the economy but that are not so severe as to trigger major instabilities. Other political considerations also enter in. Foreign pressures, whether from the United States and Japan directly or from the IMF and the World Bank, generate a nationalistic reaction among those who believe the Philippines should not submit to pressure from the institutions of the rich countries.

There is little active controversy within U.S. military circles on the strategic importance of the Philippine bases, but there is concern that deteriorating economic and political conditions in the country could make their retention increasingly difficult. In the eyes of the U.S. military and strategists, the significance of the bases has been enhanced by increased U.S. interests in the Indian Ocean and Persian Gulf and by Soviet access to facilities in Vietnam. Under an agreement concluded in January 1979, the status of the Philippine basis is reviewed every five years and after 1991 is subject to termination on one year's notice. Although it is not officially considered rent, the United States provides substantial amounts of military and economic aid to the Philippines under these agreements. The 1979 package stipulated $500 million in security assistance for fiscal years 1980-1984. The second agreement, negotiated in 1983, had a much higher price tag -- $900 million for fiscal years 1985-89, on easier terms.

Those in the United States who would like to scale down or eliminate U.S. bases in the Philippines argue that a U.S. security presence is no longer needed in Southeast Asia or that the strategic advantages conferred by the bases are not worth the price that must be paid to a corrupt and repressive regime. They maintain that the military presence creates resentments within the Philippines, makes the United States a target of nationalistic or anti-Marcos attacks, and encourages the growth of local radical groups. Despite these doubts, the dominant U.S. view supports the continuation of the bases as an integral part of the military support structure for U.S. regional and global foreign policy. It is also argued that this presence is welcomed by the other ASEAN governments and that most of the local sources of irritation at the bases have been defused by past base agreements.

Although Philippine opposition groups on the left naturally regard the U.S. bases in the Philippines as instruments of U.S. dominance, there is also a significant strand of opposition to the bases among moderate nationalists, which was articulated as early as the 1950s. Domestic critics have argued that the bases involve the Philippines in U.S. global quarrels and afford little or no protection to the Philippines from the more imminent threats it faces from insurgencies or from a potential clash with Vietnam over claims in the South China Sea.

The weakening of the Marcos regime raises difficult questions for both United States and Japanese policy. Is Marcos likely to remain in power until the next scheduled presidential election in 1987, and, if so, will he act in a manner conducive to the preparation of meaningful elections and a smooth transition of leadership? Will the political and economic crisis in the Philippines continue to grow, and, if so, how long can Japan and the United States continue to support the Marcos government without jeopardizing their ability to get along with its successors? Does the more friendly political opposition led by members of the traditional elite, such as the Aquino family, represent an effective and viable alternative to the present government? How does current U.S. and Japanese policy affect the protection of longer-term, concrete economic and political interests of both countries in the Philippines? American and Japanese policymakers probably have different assessments of the answers to these questions, and this could lead to a further complication -- the extent to which two countries can coordinate their Philippines policies and actions.

A Pacific Economic Community

Relations among the ASEAN countries, Japan, and the United States are usually conducted through bilateral channels. Few mechanisms exist for multilateral consultations, despite the growth in regional interdependence. One proposal, originating in Japan and attracting adherents in the United States, is that there should be some kind of regional organization -- a Pacific Economic Community or an Organization for Pacific Trade and Development -- that would associate the ASEAN countries with the developed countries of the Pacific and assure ASEAN periodic access to U.S. and Japanese policymakers. Such an organization, according to its adherents, would help focus public attention in the larger countries on their growing stake in the ASEAN region. This proposal, although having some supporters with ASEAN, has been coolly received in the region because of fears that a new organization would overwhelm the identity of ASEAN, associate ASEAN too closely with the West in global political rivalries, and even result in increased domination in the region by the United States and Japan, however good the intention of its founders.

Because of their own felt need for increased access to U.S. and Japanese policymakers, the ASEAN governments have initiated the expanded foreign ministers meetings that annually bring together the ASEAN foreign ministers with the U.S. secretary o state; the foreign ministers of Japan, Australia, New Zealand, Canada; and a ministerial representative from the European Economic Community. This regular consultation, which involves meetings among the entire group as well as between each minister and his ASEAN hosts, serves as a forum that the ASEAN ministers, in a sense, control. In 1984, it was agreed that these consultations, without the European representative, could serve as a venue for the discussion of general issues of Pacific Basin economic cooperation.

How adequate this will be remains to be seen. The ASEAN countries, of course, do not expect the United States and Japan to completely reorient their foreign policies toward ASEAN and subordinate their global policies to ASEAN preferences and interests. At the same time, they hope for more attention from their larger partners and particularly for increased sensitivity to the consequences on ASEAN of their global policies and bilateral relations. Japan and the United States also want to increase their associations with the dynamic ASEAN and broader Asia-Pacific regions. Therefore the further evolution of institutional mechanisms for consultation can be expected to continue to be an item for dialogue among the three sides of the United States -- Japan -- ASEAN triangle.

Ross, GARNAUT, ed. ASEAN in a Changing Pacific and World Economy, Canberra: Australian National University Press, 1980.

Lawrence B. KRAUSE. U.S. Economic Policy toward the Association of Southeast Asian Nations: Meeting the Japanese Challenge, Washington, D.C.: The Brookings Institution, 1982.

Charles E. MORRISON and Astri SUHRKE. Strategies of Survival: the Foreign Policy Dilemmas of Smaller Asian States, New York: St. Martin's Press, 1978.

NARONGCHAI Akrasanee, ed. ASEAN-Japan Relations: Trade and Development, Singapore: Institute of Southeast Asian Studies, 1983.

Guy J. PAUKER, Frank H. GOLEY, Cynthia H. ENLOE. Diversity and Development in Southeast Asia, New York: McGraw-Hill Book Company, 1977.

Robert PRINGLE. Indonesia and the Philippines: American Interests in Island Southeast Asia, New York: Columbia University Press, 1980.

Research Institute for Peace and Security. Asian Security 1984, Tokyo: 1984. (annual publication)

Sueo SEKIGUCHI, ed. ASEAN-Japan Relations: Investment, Singapore: Institute of Southeast Asian Studies, 1983.

Masahide SHIBUSAWA. Japan and the Asian Pacific Region, London: Royal Institute of International Affairs, 1984.

Lea E. WILLIAMS. Southeast Asia: A History, New York: Oxford University Press, 1976.

John WONG. ASEAN Economies in Perspective: A Comparative Study of Indonesia, Malaysia, the Philippines, Singapore and Thailand, London: The MacMillan Press, 1979.

ABOUT THE AUTHOR

Charles E. Morrison is Research Fellow at the East-West Center and Scholar-in-Residence at the Japan Center for International Exchange. He received his Ph.D. from the Johns Hopkins School of International Studies, where he also taught Southeast Asian International Relations from 1977 to 1980. He has served as a research adviser to the Japan-U.S. Economic Relations Group and to the U.S.-Japan Advisory Commission. He has authored a number of articles and books on Southeast Asian affairs, including <u>Strategies of Survival</u> (St. Martins Press, 1978, with Astri Suhrke).

DATE DUE

DEMCO 38-297